Organic Prayer

Other books by Nancy Roth

The Breath of God
A New Christian Yoga
We Sing of God: A Hymnal for Children
Praying: A Book for Children

Nancy Roth

Organic Prayer

Cultivating Your Relationship with God

Illustrations by
Susan Mangam

COWLEY PUBLICATIONS
Cambridge ✦ Boston
Massachusetts

International Standard Book Number: 1-56101-077-4
Library of Congress Number: 93-12653

Cover Illustration by Susan Mangam

Library of Congress Cataloging-in-Publication Data
Roth, Nancy, 1936--
  Organic prayer: cultivating your relationship with God/Nancy Roth; drawings by Susan Mangam.
    p. cm.
  ISBN 1-56101-077-4
  1. Prayer. 2. Human ecology—Religious aspects. 3. Gardens—Religious aspects. I. Title.
BL560.R585 1993
248.3'2—dc20   93-12653

This book is printed on recycled, acid-free paper and was produced in the United States of America.

Lyrics to the song "To My Old Brown Earth" are reprinted by permission of Pete Seeger. All scriptural quotations are taken from the New Revised Standard Version.

Cowley Publications
28 Temple Place
Boston, Massachusetts 02111

To Lee Brunner
December 27, 1950–June 11, 1992
our friend and brother in God

Acknowledgments

I wish to thank my husband, who helped this book come to fruition through his support, both domestic and literary; our son Christopher, a committed environmentalist, who first opened my eyes to the importance of this subject and provided valuable comments on the manuscript; my good friend and sensitive editor, Cynthia Shattuck; Sister Susan John Mangam, STR, with whom this book was truly a collaboration in the spirit; and, last but not least, all of God's creatures who inspired it in the first place.

Table of Contents

Foreword

BY MADELEINE L'ENGLE

When I returned from a trip of almost three weeks to Antarctica, there in the mountain of mail awaiting me was Nancy Roth's manuscript. How very appropriate it seemed to me to turn to a book on the care and nurture of planet earth just after I had spent marvelous and amazing time on a continent where the earth was still what it had been created to be!

Those of us traveling on our little ship were told by our lecturers that while we might arrive on Antarctica thinking of ourselves as tourists, we would leave thinking of ourselves as ambassadors. The word "pilgrim" was not used, but surely it would have been the right one. We went on a pilgrimage to a lost ice age, and we returned home as pilgrims awed and humbled by what we had seen. The beauty of this southernmost continent defies description. Photographs cannot show the dignity of the towering icebergs nor catch the amazing blue that makes the sky seem pale. Penguins, whales, seals, sea birds—we watched the great chain of life in all its purity and ruthlessness.

Much of what I learned on this trip to what used to be called the Antipodes is beautifully expressed in Nancy Roth's new book. I visited the Antarctic with all my senses, as Nancy encourages us to do wherever we are on planet earth—although one thing I was not prepared for was the smell! The smell of guano, the bowel movement of the penguin, is not something anyone would want to bottle and bring home. It is not a bad smell, because it is not putrefying or rotting, but it is certainly strong. Guano is pink if the penguins' diet is predominantly krill and white if predominantly fish. There is more krill than there used to be because today there are fewer whales, and the terrible loss of whales has, ironically, arrested the decline of the penguin population; there is plenty for penguins to eat.

As Nancy Roth points out, all life lives at the expense of other life. What we take from our planet, we must give back. As Scripture says, we die and are returned to the earth.

Yes, she reminds us, our *adamah*, our mortal flesh, dies and becomes once again part of the great cycle. But our *ruach*, the life-giving breath that pulses through all creatures, is eternal; it will become part of that marvelous paradox Paul calls the "spiritual body." While flesh and spirit are still intermingled, we are to honor and enjoy our human bodies and the planet on which we live.

What she has to say about our consumer society also struck a responsive chord within me. Can one be both a Christian and a consumer? I doubt it. We are meant to be nourishers, caring for our earth, not consumers. This book will help to reawaken our responsibility to all the wonders God has given us.

Prayer rocks are part of my life, too, and it is good to encounter the use of rocks for this creative purpose in *Organic Prayer*. I have on my desk a small rock with three perfect, round holes in it, found on a beach during a drive to southern California; it is my trinitarian rock, a reminder of our trinitarian God. In the pocket of my loden coat is a small "moon stone," an oval stone, silvery white, from a beach in Ayia Napa, in Cyprus. I would have liked to have brought home a stone from the rocky beaches in Anarctica, but we were sternly warned to take nothing away, not even a pebble, nor to leave anything behind. We were to come and go, leaving everything as it was. In that dry, cold climate anything we happened to drop would take centuries to biodegrade; anything we took away might make a difference to the precarious ecology. So I left stones where they were, on the beach, for penguins to use for nesting.

It was indeed a prayer for me to see two humpback whales showing off their beautiful flukes, to look at the stark cliffs where albatrosses were nesting, to smell seals sleeping on ice floes—yes, seals smell! As I read Nancy Roth's words urging us to see, taste, smell, touch, hear, focus, and walk, I was grateful to have just come from an experience where I had taken all her urgings to heart—even if I felt a little like a penguin myself as I waddled along in heavy boots with multiple socks, lined jeans over long johns, and a great red parka over layers of sweaters!

Love, we are urged in *Organic Prayer*, love not only ourselves but our grandchildren and great-grandchildren and great-great-grandchildren. Love them by helping to leave them a planet that will be fit for them to live and love in. I am grateful that we are encouraged to believe we can make a difference. After we have accepted our share of the responsibility for what greed and carelessness have done to our planet, we can then move on to accept God's forgiveness. "As we allow the seeds of responsible action to grow in us," Nancy Roth writes, "they will push away our ignorance, or complacency, and our fear. We can discover that our active expression of kinship and love can be a form of prayer for our planet."

What a lovely book this is, written with gentleness, humor, and a deep basic toughness. Susan Mangam's pictures are more than a fitting accompaniment; they are part of the very spirit of the book.

Organic Prayer

Introduction

ORGANIC PRAYER

When my husband and I moved from a New York suburb to a rural Ohio town, we dreamed of growing vegetables in the sunniest corner of our large new back yard. A child's swing set had stood there until the previous owners dug it up and moved it out, and innumerable small feet had trampled and compacted the soil. The plot looked like a research project in the horticulture of weeds: dandelions, plantain, and crabgrass were all thriving, and when we attempted to pull them out, we concluded that our land had bred powerful mutants whose giant roots reached several feet into the earth.

Ever hopeful, we hired a local handyman with a rototiller to come in and turn over the soil. Afterwards, we had to face the difficult truth that, without a deeper digging than the rototiller's few inches, the garden would revert to its former identity as a weed patch. So we attempted to hand-dig each plantain and dandelion root, not comforted by the fact that each small piece we overlooked would become a vigorous new weed.

Next, we engaged the help of a local farmer. Three times, a truck made its precarious way through our side yard to the prospective vegetable garden and dumped a load of well-aged horse manure. In the autumn, we planted a cover crop that was "dug in" the following spring as green manure. We chose what we would grow and we planted our garden, including sunflowers and marigolds to delight the eye, invite birds, and discourage unwelcome insects. We pulled weeds, began to build a compost pile, and tried to cope with insects, drought, and the appetite of a large brown rabbit who resided nearby. Our harvest included the best lettuce and the juiciest tomatoes we had ever eaten, to say nothing of enough basil to make pints of pesto for the freezer, a taste of summer in winter.

Our garden is an organic garden. We have tried to co-operate with nature through observing and using nature's own methods. We are mere beginners, but we are learning. And we are learning more than gardening. We are learning about ourselves, and about our relationship with the natural world and with God.

As I kneel at the edge of the vegetables, plunging my hands into the soil, I am also learning new things about prayer. I am learning that nature itself prays by being absolutely true to itself—"Glorify the Lord, all ye works of the Lord!"—and that being true to myself is a way of prayer. The garden is teaching me that the earth's need for healing demands my intercession and prayerful action. It is teaching me how to grow the seeds of hope, and how to utilize the debris of life's sorrows. It is teaching me about living and about dying. It is teaching me that my spirit flourishes when I meditate upon God's creation. It is teaching me, along with organic gardening, *organic prayer*.

"Organic prayer" offers me a helpful metaphor both for my contemplation of God and for my attempt to live in harmony with God's creation. Organic prayer, like the life it tends to produce, is rooted in the "soil" of our experience: the feel of the earth under our feet, our place as *homo sapiens* on that earth, and our intuitions of the holy. Our religious traditions were first based on such experience; when we trace the roots of these traditions, we find flesh-and-blood people working, playing, thinking, and praying. Scriptures, doctrines, rituals, and ethics are revitalized when we realize this. When we dig into the soil of experience—both our own and our ancestors'— we are likely to discover that prayer becomes natural: an "organic" response of the human being to God rather than an activity we need to be taught.

This metaphor for prayer helps me to practice contemplative gardening. When I gaze upon our vegetables and flowers, I take note that my prayer needs to be grounded in reality, that I need to be open to those gifts of God that give me life and nourishment, and that I need to guard against those sins that spoil the fertility of the earth and the well-being of its creatures.

What are some of the characteristics of such prayer? Because it springs from the reality of the human condition, it helps to integrate us as whole people—mind, heart, *and* body. It does not distract us and frustrate us with an otherworldly ideal of holiness, but helps us to discover the sacredness of our ordinary day-to-day living. It helps us to discover God's presence in new ways: within us and within nature as well as infinitely beyond us, known through creation's mysteries and miracles, from compost to columbines. It opens our hearts to compassion for the rest of God's creation, and our minds to the truth that we are all interconnected. Such prayer delights in the earth, whose breathtaking complexity and beauty is an icon of the Creator, more skillfully wrought than any Byzantine masterpiece.

An organic garden represents a middle ground between returning the land to wilderness and bulldozing it for condominiums. Ideally, it is a fruitful partnership between ourselves and nature. Similarly, organic prayer represents neither an impossible Eden nor an arrogant Babel, but a continual striving towards balance between ourselves and creation through partnership with the Creator. The harvest takes work; the work of attending throughout our lives to the need for weeding, watering, composting, and dealing with pests and the vicissitudes of weather. But every gardener knows that such work can be deeply satisfying, both for its own sake and because of the harvest that follows.

This book has been growing—organically, one might say—for many years. When I was a teenager commuting weekly from the New York suburbs for piano lessons in the city, I remember gazing out the train window and feeling depressed at the rubble beside the tracks: broken glass, abandoned automobiles, mounds of discarded rubber tires, the pervasive litter of old paper and cardboard blown by the wind. I remember becoming aware of an idea that felt totally and entirely *mine*: "What God has made is always beautiful; it is human beings who spoil it." Of course, in retrospect, I know that the thought was far from original. I also know that it represented only part of the truth, for my adolescent single-mindedness had temporarily blinded me to such projects as my mother's rose garden. But I remember the moment as vividly as if today I were feeling the motion of the train and looking through the plate glass at the ugliness outside.

That brings me to a key characteristic of "organic prayer." Organic prayer bears fruit. Such prayer inevitably brings about a raised consciousness of our place in nature, and the resulting crop will be different because we have changed our behavior.

Our back yard vegetable plot had to be dug deep so that the weeds could be uprooted; then it had to be watered, fertilized, and protected from pests. Turning away from attachment to our culture's thoughtless life-style is difficult and requires a similar process. When we weed out destructive habits and attitudes, we prepare for a healthier environment both within us and outside us.

George Maloney writes, "Man was to be healthy and full of life by breathing in the loving power of God. But man polluted his interior environment. What we see around us in the pollution of the air, the streams, rivers, lakes, and oceans, our woods and forests and countryside, and in the jungles of our cities, is but an *icon*, a dramatic image, externalized, of what man is doing within himself in the unlimited expanses of his 'inner space.'"[1]

It is interesting to note that the word "ecology" is rooted in the Greek *oikos*, a dwelling-place or home. One way to describe the goal of the human journey through life is as a search for at-home-ness: with ourselves, with other people, and with God. Our itinerary leads us to the dwelling-place God gave us: our planet earth. As we learn to love that home, we will increasingly wish to contribute to the earth's preservation and beauty rather than to despoil it. No proud homeowner is likely to spray graffiti on the white clapboard exterior of the house or dump out the garbage can in the middle of the living room carpet.

When we are asked to change our ways for the sake of the environment, we will find that the call of "duty" does not suffice. As every happy but weary parent of a newborn infant can tell you, *love* is the energy that helps us transcend our usual pursuit of comfort and convenience. As we learn to love and respect our home, our *oikos*, we will hear the call to action and prayer from our aching planet itself. The task will be full of urgency, and also full of joy, for the earth is full of the beauty of holiness, one of the revelations of God.

The book you are about to read contains a series of meditations, each one followed by "spadework"—prayer exercises that will help you to incorporate the insight of each meditation and experience more fully our earthly home. You might consider it a spiritual "gardening companion." The thematic sections parallel those in a gardening book. The first theme is attention to the *soil*: where we live (on the planet earth, at present); who we are ("earth" plus "spirit"); and how we experience God. In that soil we will plant *seeds*: kinship with creation, love, and responsibility. We will explore means of nurturing those seeds through the living *waters* of observation, listening, and participation. We will discover that nothing is, in the end, "waste material," and acknowledge the fertility bestowed by the *compost* of nature's cycles of life and death. We will confront *pests*, the blights that eat away at our hope and our energy. Finally, we will glimpse the *harvest*: the vision of a harmonious earth.

The format of this book—reflection alternating with concrete exercises—reflects my belief that we grow best when we grow as a whole, engaging not only our intellects but our hearts and our bodies. In the "spadework" section at the end of each chapter, the first section can be used either as a discussion question for group reflection or as a solitary meditation. If you are using this book alone, you may also wish to begin a companion volume, or "earth journal," in which to write your own reflections. The second "spadework" category is a prayer exercise. I urge you especially to try the exercises that engage you physically, even if the concept of body prayer is new to you.

Another impetus to prayer in this book are the drawings by Sister Susan Mangam, STR, a solitary religious and an artist. Susan lives in a simple studio/hermitage high in the Catskill Mountains. She lives through the work of her hands, as carpenter and artist. Above all, she prays. Susan lives close to nature, and much of her prayer occurs while she is walking beside the small river that refreshes the woods and meadows surrounding her home, helping the neighboring farmer to tend his animals, planting her vegetable garden, or sketching the rocks and waves of Maine's rugged coast on her regular visits there. Susan's pictures have always beckoned me into her silence and her kinship with nature, and they are an integral part of these meditations.

I hope that this book will reach many kinds of readers. Some of you may be practicing Christians: I hope that you will find *Organic Prayer* an "alternative prayer book" that will suggest new ways of relating to God. Some of you may be estranged from institutional religion: I hope that you will find in this book a way to the divine that rings true for you. Some of you may be environmental activists, battle-weary and struggling against hopelessness: I hope that you will find in these pages the seeds of hope and courage. Some of you may be religious "professionals" who are seeking a way to teach and preach about the environment from within a spiritual context: I hope that this book will become a resource.

This book is intended, not as an end in itself, but as a catalyst. I hope that it will mark the beginning of a process in which mind and heart engage in a new relationship with creation through prayer. In such prayer, we open ourselves to caring, for as we open to God in prayer—whether through words, thought, action, or silent attentiveness—God opens *us* to the concerns of the world. Slowly but surely, our sense of responsibility for the planet will grow as desire rather than duty, springing up from the roots of our loving delight in God's creation.

I

Soil

ohn Jeavons, a guru of the bio-intensive method of organic farming, said at a 1991 conference on "Earth and Spirit," "I want you all to *stop* growing *crops*." After an effective pause, he added, "Instead, you must begin growing *soil*."[2] When I heard this, I realized that Jeavons was also offering a remedy for shallow-rooted spirituality and mindless activism. "Growing soil" means tending our vegetables by paying attention to the nutrients and moisture in their soil rather than by dousing them with chemical fertilizer. It is the health of the soil that is responsible for the size of the squash, the tastiness of the tomatoes, and the sturdiness of the cucumber vines. This was made abundantly clear to us when we transplanted some of our seedlings to an unimproved section of our garden: scrawny vegetables struggled to survive in the hard cracked clay, only a few feet away from their healthier siblings.

We are in partnership with our soil. When we moved to Ohio, we found we had inherited dense clay that once formed the bottom of a receding Lake Erie. We had been accustomed to working in rich, light loam, the remnants of a leaf-carpeted forest floor. We are learning as much about clay as we can. We have come to appreciate its fertility, while attempting to lighten its density through the addition of peat moss and other organic matter. We are learning to work with it, rather than to engage in wishful thinking that it be otherwise. The soil—what we have been given—is the foundation of our garden.

So it is with prayer. Prayer based upon reality grows not out of thin air or wishful thinking, but from the soil of what *is*. The growth begins "underground," as our roots find nourishment deep in the soil of truth. We must first consider our place in creation, our identity as human beings, and our assumptions about God.

CHAPTER 1

Holy Ground

When my brothers and I were young, our family spent a week each summer at a YMCA conference center on Lake George called Silver Bay. My father began each day with a pre-breakfast swim and then spent long days in meetings with business associates. The rest of us had the freedom to revel in the beauty of the Adirondack scenery and to amuse ourselves as we chose. Swimming was our favorite occupation, but swimming for us meant more than just kicking our legs and moving our arms. It meant exploring the water and the shoreline, venturing as far as we could under the watchful eyes of the lifeguard and our mother.

Near the edge of the swimming area, we discovered a marvelous secret. We found it first with our bare feet, wading near the edge of the swimming area. Suddenly, our toes felt sand no longer, but curled into something smooth and somewhat sticky. A vein of clay! This was clay you could dig out with your hands and make into Indian bowls or small animal figures, whatever your fancy desired. There, right there, for the asking, was a bounty we had previously known only in the covered bins of the elementary school art room. We were instant sculptors, real potters. It was our secret, as yet undiscovered by the other "conference children."

In my teens, we discontinued our annual visits to Silver Bay and the clay was forgotten, tucked into a corner of the brain as hidden as the wondrous underwater vein in which we had discovered it. One September, however, thirty-five years later, I myself was invited to a conference at Silver Bay. I slipped my swimsuit into my luggage, just in case the weather was balmy. Once unpacked, I found that the lake drew me like a magnet, and the receptionist agreed to bend the no-swimming-without-a-lifeguard regulations if I agreed not to go in too deep. Bracing myself, I plunged into the cold water, swam the equivalent of a lap or two, and headed toward shore. When the water became too shallow for swimming, I put my feet down on what I expected would be the sandy bottom.

What was this substance I was stepping on? Memory flooded over me from the feet up. The vein of clay! Small child hands, shaping bowls. Our secret cache of art material! Reaching down, I gathered a fistful of the sticky substance and made a small bowl, which could not begin to contain my happy memories.

Of all our senses, it is probably the sense of touch that most helps us recognize our bond to the earth, inescapable as the pull of gravity. Recognizing this bond is like preparing the soil for the organic garden: it is the foundation upon which the rest depends. Although St. Paul may have said, "Our true citizenship is in heaven," he surely recognized earth's magnetic pull as he trudged along the dusty roads between Tarsus and Corinth. In this life, we are citizens of earth. Earth is our household; we belong here. And we are also guests: guests of the earth. We are dependent on the earth's hospitality, to warm us, to feed us, to give us a safe lodging. We are also pilgrims who know that we are in holy territory, for God is both with us in the journey and at the journey's end. The soil we tread, as we both defy and befriend the pull of gravity by lifting one foot after another through all the events of our lives, is sacred earth.

Each of us has our own collection of "walking memories" like my memory of the clay in Silver Bay. Some of my memories are of hiking on a deep and resilient bed of pine needles in a New England forest in the fragrant summer heat; gliding on cross-country skis across the glistening snow that blanketed the same terrain in the winter; going barefoot on the sole-tickling grass of my back yard and being tough enough to make it across a gravel path; prancing over the burning white sand at Jones Beach on New York's Long Island towards the welcome relief of the cool surf; leaving giant footprints along the miniature undulations of wet sand ridged by the retreating tide; jumping into a mud-puddle after a great storm, just for the fun of it, and discovering to my horror that it was full of earthworms up for a glimpse of the watery world; crackling autumn leaves under new school shoes; crunching snow under buckle-galoshes; bracing myself as I walked down the ramps sparkling with bits of mica in New York City's Grand Central Station; pacing slowly and silently on a concrete sidewalk in an affluent suburb during a prayer vigil to commemorate the victims of Hiroshima. I have walked in procession through the passages of life—down the sloped aisle of the high school auditorium, along the brick path under the memorial arch at the center of the college campus, upon the white runner rolled out upon the carpeted aisle of my parish church, on the terrazzo floors of the seminary chapel, over smooth grey stone towards the bishop standing at the far end of the world's longest Gothic cathedral.

When I think about placing one foot in front of the other across the various terrains that have formed my life's geography, I cannot help but be filled with wonder simply that there is a world through which to move and I am alive in it. I walk right into the mystery of creation. How can it be that this solidity underneath my feet once did not exist? How can it be that *I* at one time did not exist? I cannot comprehend it: all this once had no being.

This attitude of awe is a foundation for our love. Without awe, we are likely to take this earth for granted, just as we often take other people for granted until mortal illness strikes them or they move to the opposite coast. Like human friendships, our friendship with creation begins with attention. The fruit of such attention to the creation, as inevitable as the jack-in-the-pulpit springing up in our shady border each year, is amazement. When we truly allow ourselves to feel the pull of gravity and to notice the miracle of existence, what we experience is close kin to worship. Like Job, we stand rooted to the earth, lost in wonder.

> Then the Lord answered Job out of the whirlwind:...
> "Where were you when I laid the foundation of the earth?
> Tell me, if you have understanding.
> Who determined its measurements—surely you know!
> Or who stretched the line upon it?
> On what were its bases sunk, or who laid its cornerstone
> > when the morning stars sang together
> > and all the heavenly beings shouted for joy?"
> > > (Job 38:1,4-7)

Spadework

What memories do you have of your own "walking history"? Do you remember going barefoot as a child, perhaps at a beach? Do you remember wading in water? Walking in mud, or snow, or leaves?

Have you walked in procession at graduations or other special ceremonies? Have you marched in demonstrations or vigils? When have you been footsore, and when has it been a pleasure to walk?

What did each of these walking memories contribute to your understanding of your life on earth?

Take off your shoes and stand up. Close your eyes and visualize the kind of footprint you would make, noting which parts of the feet make the strongest contact with the floor. You are experiencing the pull of gravity, a sign of your bond to the earth.

Now practice a "walking meditation." This is a way of walking quite slowly and deliberately, focusing the mind by remaining thoroughly aware of the action of walking.

First, prepare yourself by noticing your body's alignment: hipbones over the front part of the feet, shoulder joints over hipbones, head held straight as if a string were attached to the top of the head, and knees relaxed. Breathe through the nostrils, breathing as if the lungs filled the whole torso. Notice the centering effect of this "abdominal breathing."

Notice the pull of gravity. It is the body's way of reminding you, "I belong here." Now shift all your weight onto the left foot, not tilting the body but centering it over the foot in a perpendicular line. Now lift the right foot, which is free, and take a step forward. Place the foot down heel first, and shift the weight slowly and deliberately to the right foot.

You can take a step forward with the left foot, which is now free, in the same manner. The sensation of walking like this is feline, and the contact of the sole of the foot with the ground is like a repeated massage.

When you have become accustomed to the rhythm of walking at this pace, notice also the rhythm of your breathing while you are walking. If it seems natural for you, try to coordinate the rhythm of the walking and the breathing.

If it is helpful, you may further focus the mind through re-peating silently a phrase that has meaning for you in relation to the exercise, such as "holy ground," or "pilgrimage."

CHAPTER 2

A Lump of Clay

The Rodin Museum at the Hotel Biron, 77 Rue de Varenne, is flooded with sunlight. During our visit to Paris, my husband and I decide to take our children to see the sculptures that fill its capacious rooms. We stroll in the manicured garden; I am scolded by a zealous curator for transgressing the admonition *"Défense de marcher sur la pelouse"* because I place one foot on the velveteen grass to balance myself while I lean over the rose garden to inhale. Our younger son, Michael, seats himself on the step below the massive, sculpture-covered *Gates of Hell* and strikes the pose of *The Thinker*, who gazes pensively down at the top of his head. Now we are inside the honey-colored building, and its tall windows are welcoming the sun.

Sculptures I recognize from art books are bathed in light: fauns, danaïds, nymphs, the prodigal son, studies for the monuments of Victor Hugo and of Balzac, studies for the tragic *Burghers of Calais*. We have just entered Gallery Four when a bright shaft of sunshine draws my attention to a dazzling white mass of marble on a low wooden table at the room's center. A hand, much larger than any human hand, emerges from the rough marble base like a plant from deep in the earth. The hand spirals around a great lump of stippled marble from which human limbs are beginning to emerge.

My guidebook tells me this is the *Hand of God*, created in 1898 and one of Rodin's most daring works. The catalog says that it breaks with tradition and speaks directly to the imagination, "conjuring up creatures emerging from primeval life substance." But I know that already—when I see the dazzling sculpture, I recognize in it my own understanding of humanity's origins.

Auguste Rodin has expressed in marble the spirit of the oldest creation story in the Hebrew tradition. When I ask the question, "Where do human beings fit in?" I keep returning to that early biblical tradition, especially as it is expressed in the second chapter of the Book of Genesis. Like the sculpture in the center of Gallery Four, verse seven of that chapter can serve as the centerpiece of an understanding of the human condition. Taut as Rodin's sculpture, the story is only twenty-eight words long in my version of the Bible. The passage is not science, but art; not history, but mystery, brooding below the surface. Like its marble counterpart, Genesis 2:7 speaks directly to the imagination. It suggests the essence of what it means to be human through a metaphor that, as we chisel into it, reveals stratum after stratum of meaning.

In the story in Genesis 2, God is a sculptor, forming a human shape from the *adamah*, or earth. At first the clay figure is inanimate. Then into its nostrils God breathes *ruach*, life-giving breath. The breath courses through the earth-sculpture, bringing it to life as *adam*—literally, an "earthling." *Us*. Rodin's sculpture includes both male and female bodies and that pleases me, but I also know I am included when both male and female are described as *adam*—earthling.

The story reminds me that once the *adamah* and *ruach* have intermingled, there is no longer the possibility of separation. The emotion of love releases endorphins into the bloodstream, imparting a sense of wellbeing and strengthening the immune system. The emotion of fear causes the arteries to narrow, the muscles to tense, the pupils to dilate, the heart to race. A sense of serenity raises the lactate level of the blood and anxiety causes it to fall, like a tension-barometer. What God has joined together, we have never adequately been able to put asunder, as long as we live and breathe. It is a physiological reality that our state of mind affects our body. *Ruach—* or that unseen aspect of the human person we most often describe as "spirit"—affects *adamah*, our physical selves.

Adamah affects *ruach* as well. We can swim away our anger, breathe deeply to calm our fear, and cultivate good health through loving and being loved. We can remember that a depressed state of mind and heart may sometimes be caused by fatigue or illness, and therefore become more attentive to our body's need for rest, exercise, or nourishment. It is amazing, for example, how quickly a five-mile spin on a bicycle can refresh my tired psyche and foggy brain when I have been sitting at the computer for several hours working on a manuscript.

While I am cycling, I rediscover the truth that the human person is the sum of an indivisible "body-spirit" equation: *adamah* plus *ruach* equals *adam*. That is good Hebrew theology, it was Jesus' theology, and it is also common sense: this is the way we experience ourselves. It is a pity that Christianity's view of the body has often become distorted along the course of history. I counsel many people who were taught in the name of "religion" that the body is just a necessary burden and that the Christian journey is an attempt to become more and more "spiritual," in the narrowest sense of the word. One woman recently described her body as "merely a platform for my head"! Because life continues to prove otherwise, there is a disturbing gap between what she was once told she ought to feel and her new glimpses of the body-spirit unity.

Recognizing our origins in earth and in God prepares the ground for our understanding of our place on this planet. It saves us from the terrible *hubris*, or pride, which is the source of so much of our destructiveness. When we feel disconnected from our bodies, from our earthiness, we are also disconnected from the rest of creation. But once we fully experience our own creatureliness, we can discover new pleasure in God's other creatures, animal, mineral, and vegetable. We will care about them because they are our extended family, sharing with us the molecules that make up *adamah*.

When we feel disconnected from God, from *ruach* or "spirit," we are disconnected from the very source of our being. How often we let other kinds of breath fill us—the breath of selfishness, acquisitiveness, power, greed—so that we fall prey to a kind of spiritual and moral "breathlessness." Once we begin to allow God's breath to fill us, we will find we are more human, not less so. My favorite second-century theologian, Irenaeus of Lyons, who said, "The glory of God is the human being fully alive," would have enjoyed looking over his compatriot's shoulder as Rodin chiseled the *Hand of God*.

One of humanity's most destructive misconceptions is that, since we consider ourselves the apex of creation, we are therefore separated from nature. The Judeo-Christian tradition, in its attentiveness to another verse of Genesis—"have dominion...over every living thing that moves upon the earth"—to the neglect of the wisdom contained in Genesis 2:7, has much to answer for.

We can no more be happy separated from nature than we can be happy separated from God. When we acknowledge our place on earth and celebrate our unity in God with the creation that surrounds us, we take our place in the community composed of all living things, and it feels like a homecoming.

Spadework

Are you aware of yourself as *adam*: *adamah* plus *ruach*? Have there been times in your life when you have especially felt the "body/spirit" connection?

Is there a way of prayer in which you regularly encourage that integration? Have you felt especially in touch with yourself and with God while you are outdoors, perhaps working in a garden, or walking in a park? Do you notice that exercise renews both body and mind?

Have you ever taken a class in one of the ancient body/spirit disciplines such as Tai Chi or Yoga, that can be adapted as Christian "body prayer"?

Set aside at least twenty minutes. Sit in a comfortable chair or lie down and close your eyes. Notice the tension in your muscles and gradually permit that tension to drain out of the body. In turn, relax the feet and legs, the torso, and shoulders, arms, neck, and face. Let each part of you, in turn, surrender to earth's gravity. Let go of the habitual tension of your muscles, and allow the *earth* to support you. Be aware of the heaviness of your body, a physical reminder that you are part of the earth, *adamah*.

Notice your breath entering and leaving your nostrils. Feel the life pulsing within you. Your breath is a reminder of *ruach*, God's life-giving breath that is God's gift to you. You share the renewing capacities of your respiratory system with the other animal denizens of our planet, from the cattle and creeping things to the birds flying above the earth across the dome of the sky.

Spend some time noticing the movement of your breathing. Calm the mind by using a focus: mental, visual, or tactile. You might wish to repeat silently a word such as "alive" or "*ruach*" or "God" with each breath. Or you may picture in your mind's eye a visual image, such as the *Hand of God* sculpture by Auguste Rodin. You may even gaze at a photograph of the sculpture. Or hold a lump of clay, such as the plasticine clay that is sold at art stores, gently molding it with your hands as it warms and becomes pliant.

After some time of silence, take a slow deep breath, and let *ruach* fill you with a sense of liveliness and peace. Take time to stretch. How good it feels to move! Touch your cheek, your hair, your hand, and feel their textures. Listen to the sounds within your own body and to the sounds around you. Finally, open your eyes and gaze around you. This is the earth, your home. It is good to be alive.

CHAPTER 3

All Things Green

ach summer, my husband and I are joined by a small band of other pilgrims in a journey to a music festival in one of the great cathedrals of England. Rather than rushing from town to town, collecting impressions like postcards, we choose to spend our time—usually a week or more—near that one cathedral. We join in the quiet morning eucharists; we revel in the soaring voices of men and boys singing evensong. We enter the cathedral in the soft morning light before the tourists come and again as the afternoon sun streams in the west window. And slowly the cathedral begins to grow on us—organically, as it were. We have discovered that, as our friendship with the cathedral increases, so does our sense of mystery and of God's presence, enhanced by centuries of worship and history.

One summer morning in Salisbury, as I looked at the sunlight slanting across the Purbeck marble, I began to picture myself in a forest. Here was a great sacred grove, reaching from pavement to capital. The energy of those columns held the building up, reaching from the ground right up to the vaulting, as a trunk supports its leafy canopy. These graceful marble presences supported the roof so that we would be protected from rain and snow.

Was the cathedral, I wondered, a reminder that the medieval builders' distant ancestors worshiped in the protecting shade of verdant woodland? Was I actually sitting in a temple to pantheism or childhood nature-mysticism, thinly disguised for the purposes of Christian worship?

I pictured myself as a twenty-year-old student visiting Blarney Castle on a trip to Ireland during my junior year abroad. After performing the customary ritual of dangling upside down over the parapet to kiss the Blarney Stone, my ankles securely clutched by the castle caretaker, I took a walk in the castle's woodsy environs. My path led to a magnificent circle of great oaks, so thick that they created an instant dusk. Moss carpeted the forest floor, and, since this was long after tourist season, there was a deep silence. Close to the trunk of the largest oak, I could make out a sign: "Druid Grove." That grove was not difficult to conjure up, sitting inz the slanting shadows of Salisbury Cathedral.

When I was a child, I spent long hours exploring the woods near our home. I was exhilarated by the jumble of trees, moss, ferns, and toadstools, so different from our neat suburban neighborhood. I watched the creatures who inhabited the woods: the birds, rabbits, squirrels, the water-spiders and minnows in the brook that babbled between the rocks. It seemed an enchanted place. When I was given watercolors for my birthday, I took them to the woods one day and, dipping my brushes in the brook, tried to paint the scene. It was impossible. There was too much mystery there. I realized that the scene was more than I could paint because there was more there than I could see.

Those childhood woods were not difficult to remember, sitting in the dappled sunlight of Salisbury Cathedral. Was I really, if one scratched the surface, a druid, a pagan, despite my clerical collar and my recitation of the Christian creeds? Where, I wondered, were the prayers and the theology that expressed the earthy, forest mystery so close to me in my childhood, at Blarney Castle, and in Salisbury at that very moment?

And then I remembered the Abbess Hildegard of Bingen. Hildegard grew up in the fertile Rhineland eight centuries ago. Very early in life God came to her while she was at prayer, through visions that taught Hildegard about God, deepening and expanding the theology she was learning from her teachers, the holy nun Jutta and the Benedictine monks who lived in the monastery next door.

Hildegard found the courage to express her visions in writings illustrated by "illuminations," bold paintings in which she struggled to convey what she had seen. She wrote poetry and composed music full of originality. The abbess became known as "the Sibyl of the Rhine" and her counsel was sought by clerics and popes, kings and queens, nuns, monks, and laypeople. Hildegard was a living example of the theory that, in the theological enterprise, prayer is the equivalent of original research in the scientific community.

There was no word that could quite express what Hildegard understood about God, so she made one up: *viriditas*. *Viriditas* reminded her of *viridis*, the color of green plants. *Viriditas* was the power for growth, the luxuriant energy of the spirit of God. That was what Hildegard had learned on her childhood ramblings. So she also had been a fledgling druid! She had experienced God in a pentecostal surging right through the soles of her feet, nurturing her just as God nurtured the vines and trees and grasses among which she walked. For Hildegard, God was organic, full of the energy of good rich compost.

Hildegard sees salvation history in terms of *viriditas*. In a poem to Mary, the mother of Jesus, she sings,

> Hail to you, O greenest, most fertile branch!
> You budded forth amidst breezes and winds
>   in search of the knowledge of all that is holy.

When the time was ripe
    your own branch brought forth blossoms....
In you, the most stunning flower has blossomed
    and gives off its sweet odor
    to all the herbs and roots,
    which were dry and thirsting before your arrival.
Now they spring forth in fullest green![3]

When Hildegard's spirit felt dry and sterile, God's dew, God's moisture made her feel alive again, so she could in turn nourish others. It is no wonder that this understanding of God revealed itself in her visions, the language of Hildegard's unconscious and of her half-forgotten childhood memories:

I am the breeze that nurtures all things green.
I encourage blossoms to flourish with ripening fruits.
I am the rain coming from the dew
    that causes the grasses to laugh
    with the joy of life.[4]

Hildegard expresses articulately for Christians the *immanence* of God: God's real presence in and through creation. The great teacher of prayer Evelyn Underhill saw the contemplation of nature as the first step towards a relationship with God: "To elude nature, to refuse her friendship, and attempt to leap the river of life in the hope of finding God on the other side, is the common error of a perverted mysticality....So you are to begin with that first form of contemplation which the old mystics sometimes called the 'discovery of God in His creatures.'"[5]

In contemplating God in creation, however, we are contemplating One who is also *beyond* creation; one of the splendors of this theology is that the creation reflects the divine transcendence. Hildegard, who had such brilliant visions of the heavenly choirs, "[persisting] strongly in the way of truth as they sang the praises of the city of celestial joy," would find it difficult to accept the notion of immanence without this sublime counterbalance.[6]

Hildegard experienced God through *viriditas*, which adds to the language of Christian spirituality a marvelous new expression for the activity of God's Spirit. Hildegard would probably insist that one can know God through the soles of the feet, walking a woodland path cushioned with seasons of fallen leaves or on a sandy seashore with the waves lapping at the toes. Or when plunging the hands deep into rich earth, energized through the soil, moving out of ordinary time. I experience this other dimension of time when I am gardening; it is only dusk that finally attracts my attention, forcing me to peer in the window at the kitchen clock and, wondering where the time has fled, to run inside to wash up and start dinner.

The shadowy druid grove, the woods of childhood memory, the *viriditas* of Hildegard's lush Rhineland and—not surprisingly, after all—the great stone columns of the medieval cathedral all express in their particular ways a God who sustains and surrounds us, from the soles of the feet right on up, through creation as well as beyond creation. As we dig the foundations of our organic garden of prayer, we need to comprehend this truth.

Spadework

Have you ever had a sense of God's immanence in the natural world as described in this chapter? What aspects of the natural world? An awe-inspiring view, such as Arizona's Grand Canyon, the New England seacost, or the Swiss Alps? The sight of billowing clouds from the vantage point of a window seat on an airplane? The Milky Way on a clear night?

Or perhaps it is the delicate complexity of nature that most fully reveals God to you. A single squash seed growing, miraculously, into yards of twining green stem? The blue beauty of a single cornflower blossom? The iridescent wings of a dragonfly?

Take a walk in a woods, in a park, or along a tree-lined street. As you walk, try to be aware of the weight of your body shifting from foot to foot, and the contact of each foot with the ground.

Then choose a particular tree and notice it carefully. Touch the bark. Is it rough or smooth? Does it have a pattern? Are there marks in it that suggest some of the tree's history—a broken limb, a scar from a bolt of lightning, holes made by insects or woodpeckers, initials cut with a pocketknife?

Look up. Can you see the top of the tree? How tall is it in relation to the other trees and buildings around it? How tall is it in relation to you?

What is the shape of the tree? Round, fan-shaped, pyramidal?

Are there many small branches, or several large strong ones?

Does the tree seem healthy or unhealthy?

Is it an evergreen? Are there needles? In what pattern do the needles grow?

Or is it deciduous? If it is late winter, can you see the buds yet? If it is spring, are the leaves unfolding? Are they the yellow-green of spring or the darker green of summer? Are they beginning to turn to autumn colors? What colors? Or is the tree bare?

Picture the roots, reaching deep into the ground. Can you see evidence of the roots nearby—a cracked flagstone in the sidewalk, perhaps, or a mound in the grass? How deep and how wide do you imagine the roots reaching? Can you picture them drawing nutrients and moisture from the earth, giving energy and growth to the tree?

CHAPTER 4

Rocks

first saw the landscape of the American West from the window of an airplane. It took my breath away. Living for most of my life on the east coast, I had never gazed upon such dazzling geology. The reds and oranges of a New England autumn had transmigrated to the rocks of Utah. The rocks appeared permanent and eternal, the skeleton of a continent, holding together the land like Israel's God, her rock and her redeemer.

Wherever I travel, I pick up rocks. As my luggage gets heavier, my storehouse of memories grows. A gnarled, silvery-green rock from above the tree line in Switzerland. A scrap of chalk from England's Channel cliffs. Flint found lying beside a Roman wall in Canterbury. A pebble plucked from the shifting sands around France's Mont-Saint-Michel.

A friend, guessing my affinity for these tangible reminders, gave me my first "prayer rock." A rosy beige like the desert sand, smoothed by centuries, it fits perfectly into the palm of my hand. She found it, she told me, on the shore of the Sea of Galilee. When I hold this rock, shaped by the water that washes through the gospel stories of Jesus, it is a foundation stone in my prayer. When my thoughts want to wing elsewhere, it is a weighty reminder of what I am supposed to be doing.

My second prayer rock was the gift of Wayne, a talented baritone who had been stricken with AIDS. Wayne met with a weekly meditation group in his apartment and one day he offered us his cherished collection of rocks as a meditative focus. The next week, he told me he wanted me to choose one to keep. I chose a jagged crystal clouded with veins of white and midnight blue, which reminded me of the valley of shadows through which Wayne was passing.

I began to use my rocks as an intercession list. When I prayed for Wayne, I held the blue crystal. When I wished to hold the suffering world before God, I held the rock shaped smooth by the Sea of Galilee, on whose shores once walked the Prince of Peace.

Susan, deep in the happy travail of creating this book with me, brought me a sea-green stone shaped by the surf along the Maine coast. It is a rock washed by layers of color and mottled with small crevices, a rock suggesting the hidden resources of its giver, an artist and a contemplative.

For many years after my ordination, I often worked in tandem with my colleague, Lee. When we created dance and movement workshops together, they flowed effortlessly out of our similar vision: helping people to engage both body and breath in responding to the mystery of God. When I knew I would be moving five hundred miles away from Lee, I begged him for a rock; typically, he sent not one but two. One is small, simple, and silvery, discovered on the "dancing ground" of an early Shaker community in Massachusetts. He picked up the other rock near the entrance to the Ellora Caves in India. One side of that stone is rough and undistinguished, but overturned, it is the castle of crystal described by St. Teresa, sparkling and vivacious.

More and more my prayer is built upon these rocks my friends have given me. They connect my body to these other bodies, healthy or ill, living this life or living in life eternal.

They are so solid, so real. They contribute a focus to prayer I have found in no other way.

When prayer is difficult, any rock will do. As I hold it in my hand, its weight centers me. When I am at a loss for words, I need only hold this symbol of my intercession.

Sometimes the rocks in my collection have themselves become part of the drama that suggests a pattern in life's chaotic landscape. The rocks from Lee arrived on a day when I was attending a conference on story-telling. At midday, I had returned home for lunch and discovered the package on top of the morning's mail. Nestled within were Lee's contributions to my prayer: the silvery Shaker sliver and the crystalline Indian geode. When I returned to the conference, there on the carpet, right in the middle of our circle of chairs, a circle of rocks lay. "Take a rock, hold it in meditation, and let it evoke a story from you," we were instructed. Was this a chapter from a science fiction novel, or was it, instead, the mystery of life's interconnections shining through the veil that usually hides it?

In our old garden in New York, turning over the soil in the spring produced a veritable harvest of rocks. Here in northern Ohio, growing vegetables on what was once a lake bottom, I miss the rocks and may eventually need to import some. Without rocks and smaller pebbles, the soil drains poorly and some local gardeners purchase bags of small stones to add to their gardens along with the manure and peat moss. I like rocks to walk upon or to place as solid accents amongst the foliage. I also like to place in the garden the larger cousins of those rocks I use in my prayer.

I am making a beginning already. An old family friend in New Hampshire gave me one of two volcanic rocks that were a gift from a weather observer at a station in the Antarctic. Sitting in my garden like a large black Swiss cheese, this rock will remind me of the icy world so many miles from me where the earth is still what it was created to be, and of my responsibility to do all I can to protect it. Recently, I hauled home five flat pieces of slate from the brook running across the back of my mother's property. As I step on them, bending over to pluck flowers or to pull weeds, I remember to be thankful that she has had many happy years near that brook, and that she has lived such a long and fruitful life.

My rocks connect me to my friends, both the living and the dead. The stories behind them suggest a pattern that is a glimpse of the kingdom of God. They are the signs of the One who is permanent, in the midst of all life's transitions. They remind me, with the Psalmist, that God is my rock and my refuge, the rock of my strength and my redeemer.

Spadework

Make a list of words that come to mind for you when you think of "rock."

In what sense is God like a rock? Is there any connection in your mind or experience between "rock" as a noun and "rock" as a verb? Does the strong rock of your salvation also "rock" you in a maternal embrace? Are there times when you have felt called by your conscience to "rock the boat"?

Choose a rock from outdoors (or perhaps you too have a collection) and hold it in your hand. Close your eyes and feel its weight. Does it feel cool? Notice as you hold it that the rock gathers warmth from your body heat. Feel its texture. Is it rough or smooth? Does it have any sharp edges? What is its shape? Has it been rounded by the waves of the ocean or the water of a river? Is it flat and layered, like shale? Is it angular and irregular? Get acquainted with this ordinary object from nature that you are holding.

Then permit the rock's uniqueness to become apparent. How old do you think it is? How old are you? How does the comparison make you feel? Does the rock seem very permanent in comparison to a human life? If the rock could tell the story of what it has seen, what might it tell about the ages of the earth?

What thoughts come to your mind when you consider the rock as an icon, a "window" to the divine? Does this particular rock remind you of someone for whom you wish to pray? Does this rock remind you of the earth's "skeleton," connecting you to others as deeply as bedrock? Does it remind you of God, the Rock upon whom you can depend?

Do you remember Matthew's parable of the wise man who built his house upon rock? "The rain fell, the floods came, and the winds blew and beat on that house, but it did not fall, because it had been founded on rock" (7:26).

Hold the rock in the palm of your hand, and let the strong images inspired by this ordinary—yet extraordinary—natural object become part of your prayer.

II.

Seeds

Soil is the foundation of a garden. It is the reality supporting the flowers and fruits that spring from it. My own garden reality is clay, to which I have added manure, peat, and sand.

The soil, or foundation, from which prayer springs is the understanding that we are body-spirit, formed from the earth and from the breath of God. Along with the planet's other creatures, we have for a time been given the earth as our beloved home, and we can know God, in part, in and through the earth itself.

The soil alone does not a garden make, however. There would be little activity in our vegetable plot if we had not planted it with seeds. Early each spring, we ask ourselves the question, "What do we want to grow?" We browse through garden catalogs. Then we buy seeds, press them one by one into the soil, and water and tend them until they sprout into the plants that will feed and delight us.

Thinking about soil and seeds, I look at the life of prayer. We can claim a marvelously fertile philosophy, but our prayer is barren if we do not plant and cultivate some of the attributes that grow into meaningful life for ourselves and for others.

When we choose seeds for the garden, we choose the plants we will need during the coming season. Since we are inordinately fond of pesto, we plant basil. We plant tomatoes, lettuce, and cucumbers because nothing compares with a salad plucked fresh from the garden a few minutes before the meal. We plant melons and winter squash for the long haul.

We could have chosen others, but these are what our family needs. In the same way, choosing the seeds that we will nurture through our prayer is best done through thinking about what the earth family needs. If I were leafing through the quality-of-life catalogs, I would chose three kinds of seed to begin with: the seeds of kinship, love, and responsibility. These three are eminently suited to the soil in which we plant them, and we will find that as they grow and flourish, each has the capacity to grow like the mustard seed of Jesus' parable, contributing nourishment, shelter, and healing to God's earthly creation.

CHAPTER 5

Kinship

A mother doe and her two fawns grazed in the meadow sloping towards the river below the monastery, where my friend Lee, mourning the recent death of a friend, had sought the quiet of a long retreat. Suddenly, the silence was pierced by inhuman screaming. Through the window of his cell, Lee saw one of the young fawns being attacked by a pack of wild dogs.

Running outdoors, he met the monastery's prior also running towards the meadow. By the time they reached the fawn, the creature's hind section had been so badly torn open that it was unable to stand. While the prior called the veterinary hospital, Lee stroked the fawn's soft spotted coat, pulsating with labored breathing, and tried to reassure the creature that it was in safe hands. With a sheet for a sling, they carried the fawn to the car for the journey to the veterinarian, but their efforts failed: the fawn died from loss of blood before they arrived.

The following evening, Lee observed his daily ritual of walking down to the river to watch the sunset. Climbing back up the hill to the monastery in the dusk, he heard something moving through the forest that stretched along the river bank. He thought of picking up a stick in case it turned out to be the wild dogs, this time in search of larger prey, but then he saw her, in a clearing under the tall pines. Rather then fleeing, the mother doe looked at Lee.

Without speaking a word, Lee gestured with his hands to convey the opening of his heart to her in compassion, silently trying to share his own grief with her. At that precise moment, as if she had just learned of the fawn's fate, the doe began pounding the earth, mournfully crying out loud and long. Then, rearing on her hind legs, she bounded across the open meadow to the exact spot where the injured fawn had fallen, paused, and turned her head around to look directly at her human brother before she disappeared into the woods.

Like St. Francis, who wandered the Umbrian hills in the company of Brother Sun, Sister Moon, and Mother Earth, Lee had an extended family. His love of earth's other creatures was natural and transparent, like Frederick Buechner's Anglo-Saxon monk, Godric, who said, "Five friends I had, and two of them snakes." Lee's story of the doe, extraordinary though it may seem, is a kind of icon, or opening, through which we may glimpse *everyone's* heritage of kinship with the earth's other creatures.

Such experiences of kinship help us to see with the eyes of God, whose compassion encompasses even the fall of a sparrow. They are glimpses of our connection with all of creation, like the series of paintings by the American Quaker Edward Hicks in which wide-eyed animals, from lions and leopards to lambs and cattle, cluster around a young child. These moments are the seeds that can eventually grow into a new consciousness about our place in the universe.

My own moment of truth was unexpected. I had dutifully agreed to go on a whale-watching expedition off Cape Cod with our two young sons. As the boat drew away from the dock, I found a spot on the bow so that I could enjoy the salt breeze and sunshine, enough of a reward as far as I was concerned, although I'd brought binoculars just in case we came across a whale. We had been out only about twenty minutes when it was announced that a whale had been sighted. I whipped the binoculars to my eyes, only to find that I could see nothing because of my tears. As the boat drew closer, we could observe that great creature breaching, alternately revealing and hiding its enormous body with what I could only call playfulness.

It is difficult to explain why the sight moved me so. Perhaps it was the oceanic freedom of the creature, or the fact that for once I could observe an animal in its natural environment, without barriers between us. Or that it was so *big*. Or so unafraid. All I can say is that I felt after the whale watch that I could have died content, and for one who savors living, that was a complete surprise. I suppose it was because, for the moment, life seemed utterly complete.

When the whale surfaced in the sea before us, something else became evident as well. That whale was a sacrament of kinship for me. She was an outward and visible sign through which I glimpsed another, more profound truth: the unity of all things in God. She was no abstract concept of unity. She was a real whale. Like real bread, real wine, real water of baptism. Or a real doe mourning her fawn.

Sometimes an experience of kinship is an unexpected gift, as it was in the stories I have just recounted. But we can also deliberately nurture our sense of family. More than fifty years ago, the naturalist Jacob von Uexkull coined a word, *umwelt,* to describe the world around a living thing as that creature experiences it.[7] It can be very humbling to study another species in depth, trying to enter its world by imagining life from that creature's point of view.

Your dog, for example. While your own nostrils have a scant five million cells that sense smell, a dog's nose has anywhere from 125 to 300 million—and they are more efficiently located. We cannot hold our heads too high when we reflect on the fact that dogs have noses that are a million times more sensitive than ours. Can you imagine being able to find the one stick thrown by your owner into the brush-strewn vacant lot just by sniffing?

Or imagine living as an ant, spending your whole life in a small corner of a field of blossoms. You communicate with your friends and co-workers through the vibrations felt through the earth, or through touching antennae. You work your way through grass, flower stems, particles of dirt, and pebbles as human beings would hike through a forest strewn with boulders.

We might find that we envy the skills of our animal kin. I suspect my mother might have wished she had the sensory equipment of a bat on the afternoon that my two-year-old brother wandered off while she was shopping in the cavernous Marshall Field department store in Chicago. Because he was shorter than the tops of the merchandise display counters, it seemed an eternity before he was found strolling the aisles, oblivious to the crisis he had caused. The bat mother, on the other hand, entering a nursery cave where thousands of mother and baby bats cling to the wall or wing through the air, zeroes in on her one infant, having located it by calling to it and smelling a path to it.[8]

A spider recently wove her residence between the legs of our charcoal grill and the garage wall. Because I hoped that her progeny would be useful allies in our annual summer struggle with the mosquito population, and because her web was in such a precarious spot, I made it a point to observe her daily. At first, all I observed in the web, besides the spider and a few insect carcasses, were three round brown egg cases about the size of peas. When one of them appeared to have exploded into small pin-points, I peered very closely and recognized tiny wiggling miniatures of the mother. Almost immediately, however, they clustered together, immobile.

I discovered, later, the reason; they had received a sharp command from their mother, who had perceived me as dangerous:

> The web serves as a telegraph line by which various messages can be perceived. All web spiders live in a tactile world....The spider mother has a standardized warning signal....While the movements used to call her young make the web vibrate slightly and softly, warning is given by a short, violent jolt to the web caused by rapid movement of a hind leg....This warning serves to send forward youngsters...back to the safe hiding place.[9]

Because the spider's perception of time must be so finely tuned, it can perceive vibrations beyond the reach of a snail, for whom any fast motion is perceived as stationary. Despite the fact that we are quicker than snails, I suspect that most human observers would also find it difficult to interpret the mother spider's signals.

Close observation of other species is a good antidote to our customary human arrogance. As we share the suffering of the doe or the gladness of the whale, or as we notice the wondrous gifts God has bestowed upon creatures other than ourselves, our sense of family, or "kin," will begin to expand. We might take note that the word "kin" contributed its root to a description of human behavior known as "kindness." The seeds of our kinship will, ultimately, grow into kindness, nurtured by our respect for all members of the extended family of God's creatures upon earth.

Spadework

Observe or study another species in order to imagine what it is like to experience life from that animal's point of view. What do things *look* like, *smell* like, *feel* like, *sound* like? Are you large or small? What is your perception of space and time?

Take, for example, the spider—a creature commonly discovered sharing our homes with us. What would it be like to experience life's events—a meal, a courtship, the waywardness of our children—through the subtle movement of a fragile web? What would it be like to inhabit a world in which our dwelling place was the product of our own body, constantly subject to the vagaries of fate in the form of stiff breeze or a large human being deciding to move the barbecue grill?

When you begin to enter another species' world in your imagination, you are likely to find, as I did, that you begin to care about them. I no longer protect the spider family merely because of their usefulness to me, but because I recognize that they have integrity in their own right, as part of creation. A quick personal test of environmental consciousness is to ask yourself the question, "What do I do when I find a spider in my home? Do I squash it, leave it in peace, or move it carefully outside?"

Include other species in your prayers. You may pray especially for the particular species you have chosen to observe and study, whether they be the denizens of a rainforest or animals who live near you or with you.

You may especially wish to include some endangered species in your intercessions. Pray for them just as you pray for members of the human family who are in need. One way to do this is silently to "hold before God" the creatures for whom you are praying. Or you may repeat their names, like a litany: "Creator God, protect and preserve the spotted owl...the humpback whale...the timber wolf...the peregrine falcon...the rhinoceros...the whooping crane...the tiger...the gorilla...the manatee...."

In penitence and sorrow, on behalf of the human family, hold before God those species who are extinct, especially on account of human destructiveness.

ove

 had been invited by the rector of a comfortable suburban parish to preach a children's sermon on the theme of love, followed by a homily for adults. Searching for a concrete illustration of the theme, I found among the treasures in my attic a box containing three milk-weed pods almost ready to burst open. I took it out and wrapped it up with colorful paper and ribbon.

When the time came for the sermon, I gathered the children around me, sat down on the chancel steps, and whisked the box out from under my vestment. I told my captive audience that I was going to tell them about love.

What was in the box? I asked them. A gift. A gift that reminded me of love.

They helped unwrap it. Out came the pods. Freed from confinement, they finally burst open and hundreds of white silken parachutes drifted upwards with their cargo of seeds, aided and abetted by puffs of breath from the excited children. After that, I didn't need to say very much. They would remember that love is discovered in the giving, and setting it free is the way it reaches out to the world. I am quite sure most of them realized that if the church floor had been garden soil, each parachute would have had the opportunity to drop its seed and so fulfill its function as airborne transportation for a planting project.

When I got to my feet and ascended the pulpit for the adult homily, I found I was gazing out over a veritable snowstorm of milkweed parachutes, wafting their brown seed passengers over the heads of the congregation, dancing in the light of the blue and gold stained glass, and hovering in landing patterns over the dark red plush carpeting that covered the aisles. I reflected, gazing at the sight, that once love is set loose in bounteous freedom, it is difficult to capture it back for ourselves, even for the sake of whoever might have the job of vacuuming after Sunday services.

How can we nurture, and then learn to set free, the love that in some ways is so natural to us and in other ways so difficult? Once we acknowledge our kinship with earth's other creatures, what does it mean to love them?

When one of the Pharisees asked Jesus, "Teacher, which commandment in the law is the greatest?", he responded by citing the great ethical code of Judaism: "'You shall love the Lord your God with all your heart, and with all your soul, and with all your mind.' This is the greatest and first commandment. And a second is like it: 'You shall love your neighbor as yourself'" (Matt. 22:37-39).

The Ten Commandments help to describe these two relationships in further detail; they help us to understand that love is an action, not merely a sentiment. We love God by honoring God alone, by keeping God's name sacred, and by keeping the sabbath holy. We love others by honoring our parents and by not harming our neighbor in any way, whether through murder, adultery, lying, stealing, or covetousness. We love by respecting and by refusing to do harm.

It has been suggested that we who have such power to harm the earth need further guidance in how to love. We need an "eleventh commandment," which might be phrased something like this: "The earth is the Lord's and the fullness thereof: thou shall not despoil the earth, nor destroy the life thereon."[10] In other words, we love the earth by respecting the earth as God's creation, and by not harming it in any way.

So often we interpret Jesus' call to love in a narrow, egocentric, or even sentimental manner. We think of the way we feel about other human beings, and particularly the ones who are like us. But I think that Jesus' idea of love contains the soaring freedom of the milkweed seed. It is universal, including even people—and species—to whom we might not be naturally attracted. And it makes us want to act in such a way that we do no harm to any part of the fabric of creation.

God's love is mirrored in nature through an intricate web of connection, communication, and attraction. "Survival of the fittest" is only a subplot of the main action; the other, and larger, part of the story, is interdependence. The natural world is a symphony of symbiosis: the counterpoint of green plants and sunshine, flower and bee, earthworm and humus. Nature herself can teach us to begin to break free from human egocentricity and competitiveness.

When young children ask questions like "Does the tree hurt when you cut it down?" perhaps they are voicing their intuition that nature communicates for the purpose of mutual well-being. In 1979, Davey Rhoades, a researcher at the University of Washington, observed that when tent caterpillars attack a willow, the chemical composition of the willow's leaves changes so that they become less palatable and less digestible. The fact that the tree wishes to discourage the caterpillars' appetite for its own leaves is, perhaps, no surprise, but somehow the word gets out to the neighbors, too, possibly by the release of a chemical into the air. Other trees in the area, without any physical contact either of branches or roots, begin to produce the same defenses, and their leaves also become unpalatable. A fellow biologist, reacting to the news that it was no longer possible to view trees as passive or helpless, commented, "The theoretical basis—that it pays to eavesdrop on the troubles of one's neighbors—*is* compelling."

In another experiment, two scientists at Dartmouth College, Ian Baldwin and Jack Schultz, potted forty-five poplar plants. They placed thirty of them in one room, and the remaining fifteen in a chamber quite a distance away. Then they simulated an insect attack on fifteen of the trees in the first room by ripping the leaves with their hands, leaving the rest of the trees untouched. After two days, they analyzed the leaves, looking for specific poisonous compounds designed to ward off insects. They found that the leaves from both the ripped *and* the unripped leaves in the first room showed significant increases of these chemicals, while the leaves in the faraway chamber showed no such change. "I was home when Ian got the first results," says Schultz. He said, 'Hey, poplars talk!'"[11]

Spadework

Do you think there is a need for an "eleventh commandment" to protect the earth and everything that lives upon it? Do you think that such a commandment would suggest that we must include our behavior towards creation in our personal and institutional ethical codes?

What are some of the ways humanity has broken the eleventh commandment? How has our species despoiled the earth and destroyed life?

What are some of the ways we can respond to this new commandment through actions that contribute to the fullness of God's creation?

Take some time to become quiet and relaxed. Then think of a child whom you care about: your own child, grandchild, or a young friend. Try to see her in your mind's eye and to hear her voice. Picture her in her daily activities—school, play, meals, sleep. Picture her surroundings. What memories do you have of your friendship with this child? How does thinking about her make you feel?

Take some time to hold before God in prayer this child whom you love.

Now, in your imagination picture the child thirty or forty years hence, in adulthood, possibly with children of her own. What will their world be like? Will their surroundings—their home, their office, their school—be pleasant and safe? Will their air be clear? Will the water they drink be healthy for them? Will they be protected from the sun's rays? Will they be able to experience the wilderness? Will all the animal species of your day still share the planet with them? Picture the world you would like to see them live in.

Take some time to hold your concerns and hopes in prayer.

Finally, picture the child as an old man or woman, seventy or eighty years hence, with children and grandchildren. Again try to visualize the community in which they are living, and the state of air, water, and safety. Will there be wilderness areas? Will all the plant and animal species we know still exist?

Hold your concerns and hopes in prayer.

End by thanking God for the gifts of love and imagination, which enable you to remember the kinship and interdependence of all creatures, present and future.

Responsibility

On my first visit to Canterbury in England, I decided to spend the night in the most picturesque hotel in town, built right into the gate of the wall surrounding the cathedral close. I was given the key to a crooked room at the top of narrow stairs. Out the small window above my bed, I could see into the cathedral grounds, dark and silent, and glimpse, in the moonlight, the gray stones of the mother church of Anglicanism.

I was almost asleep when I heard the voice, a voice that made me wonder if I had traveled from the United States not only in distance but in centuries. "Eleven o'clock and all is well! Eleven o'clock and all is well!"

It was the town crier, or nightwatch, who made it possible for the citizens of Canterbury to turn over in bed and nod off, knowing that nothing sinister was afoot. That night all *was* well in Canterbury, but as I lay in bed I thought of the times when perhaps the town crier had the task of proclaiming danger. A fire in the thatch of a cottage, perhaps, or an accident in the high street. Over the centuries, the function of a nightwatch has been to be awake when others were not, to notice what was going on, and then to proclaim it at the top of his voice.

SEEDS

Town criers may no longer appear in their historic role, even in Canterbury, but we hear their voices nevertheless. "Eleven o'clock and all is *not* well. Eleven o'clock and the earth is *not* well."

None of us likes to hear those voices. Today's town criers tell us tales of holes in the ozone, habitat destruction, global warming, famine, overpopulation, toxic waste, war, pollution. The news comes to us now through different media; from long, published reports in small print to television talk shows and books with frightening titles. The cries come from people of many disciplines—scientists, sociologists, historians, philosophers, naturalists, environmentalists, artists, and clergy—who have noticed the true state of the world while the rest of us have been asleep. They are our contemporary prophets.

How loath we are to leave our beds. We rationalize. Perhaps we have heard the words incorrectly: "Perhaps the message really was, 'And all *is* well.' Perhaps it was a mistake. Perhaps it is just a false alarm. It's not happening in my street, anyway, so why worry?" Perhaps if we just roll over and go to sleep, we'll find in the morning that the voice of warning was only a nightmare.

If we go on sleeping, we'll be missing the point. For why does a town crier call out disturbing news? Is it so we can bury our heads under our pillows, to dream of a better time? Or so that we will toss and turn, frightened and sleepless with worry?

It is neither. The nightwatch's calls that all is not well are calls to *action*. We are meant to respond. Centuries ago, when a crier announced that a thatched roof in Canterbury was in flames, each able-bodied person who could carry water was important. Each pail, small as it was, contributed to the end result: the saving of a family's home. No one person could have done it alone; everyone's effort counted.

The calls of our contemporary town criers can plant the seeds of responsibility in us, if we but heed them, for they call us to work together for change. As we allow the seeds of responsible action to grow in us, they will push away our ignorance, our complacency, and our fear. We can discover that our active expression of kinship and love can be a form of prayer for our planet.

I have a friend who watches over a river. Her activity is not mere observation. Unhappy about the pollution of the river near her home, she was elated to discover that there existed a corps of volunteer "river watchers" who were assigned to check the river regularly, take water samples, report illegal dumping, and clean up trash. She tries to articulate the effect of joining the river water corps: "It begins to change the river, yes, but most of all, it changes *you*." She says that her river reminds her of Ezekiel's vision of the river that flows from the city of God:

> Wherever the river goes, every living creature that swarms will live, and there will be very many fish, once these waters reach there. It will become fresh; and everything will live where the river goes. (Ezekiel 47:9)

Sometimes we ourselves, like my friend the river-watcher, notice what needs to be done. But sometimes, when a problem is more hidden, we need to be informed. We can be grateful to those voices in our land who inform us about the deteriorating environment, because without them we might remain oblivious to the truth. And it is only through knowledge of the truth that we can respond; it is only through our response that there is hope of healing.

Our contemporary prophets call our species to repentance, just as the prophets of Israel did. In our own way we have turned away from obedience to God by disregarding the integrity of God's creation. The Hebrew prophets knew that their voices would beckon in a new age if their hearers' hearts could be turned to God. That new age would be an era full of harmony, beauty, and fruitfulness: the world as God created it to be.

> Return, O Israel, to the Lord your God,
>> for you have stumbled because of your iniquity....
> Accept what is good....
> I will be like the dew to Israel;
> he shall blossom like the lily,
> he shall strike root like the forests of Lebanon.
> His shoots shall spread out;
> his beauty shall be like the olive tree,
>> and his fragrance like that of Lebanon.
> They shall again live beneath my shadow,
> they shall flourish as a garden....
>> (Hosea 14:1,2b,5-7)

If we can be roused from our communal slumber, there will be hope of a new day for the earth. The sleep rubbed from our eyes, we can contribute to the earth's healing. We will join in common cause, like a new Israel or a reinvigorated Christian community. For the nightwatch's cry is, actually, a message from the God of Creation.

When we respond to this message and try to make room in our lives for our love of the earth to blossom into action, the selfsame voice assures us that we will not undertake the task alone.

> Then you shall call, and the Lord will answer;
>> you shall cry for help, and he will say, Here I am....
> The Lord will guide you continually,
>> and satisfy your needs in parched places,
>> and make your bones strong;
> And you shall be like a watered garden,
>> like a spring of water,
>> whose waters never fail.
>> (Isaiah 58:9-11)

Spadework

Have you heard any "town criers" lately? Perhaps you have been reading about the logging in old growth forests of the Northwest that is jeopardizing the wildlife habitat there. Or you have heard a television report about the increase in skin cancer due to the thinning of the ozone layer that protects us from the sun's ultraviolet rays. How have such messages made you feel? Frustrated? Angry? Anxious? What are some of the ways you can think of to respond to these messages?

> The kingdom of heaven is like a mustard seed that someone took and sowed in his field; it is the smallest of all the seeds, but when it has grown it is the greatest of shrubs and becomes a tree, so that the birds of the air come and make nests in its branches. (Matthew 13:31-32)

Sometimes we can feel overwhelmed when we recognize the needs of the world. It is helpful to remember that God's way is the way of growth, and that even our smallest actions can eventually bring abundant blessings to our world. For a tangible reminder of that truth, try to sprout some alfalfa seeds—like the mustard seed, it is "one of the smallest of all the seeds."

Buy some alfalfa seeds at a health food store. Soak a teaspoonful of seeds in water for a few hours in a large mason jar covered with a temporary lid you have made from cheesecloth attached with a rubber band (or perhaps you can find a lid with holes, made just for this purpose). Rinse the seeds and tip the jar on its side so that the water drains. Repeat the rinsing and draining process each morning and evening until the seeds sprout, several days later, and then refrigerate them and enjoy them as garnish or in a salad. Once you have experimented with alfalfa seeds, you may wish to use other seeds or beans, such as mung beans, for the project.

III.

Water

Once I planted some lettuce seeds and went on a journey without asking our neighbors to water them. What greeted us upon our return, after three weeks of drought, were a few scrawny leaves, hardly enough for a garnish for one serving of potato salad.

Following soil preparation and seed planting, sunlight and water are absolute requisites for our garden. I do not have any control over the former, but my continual vigilance is required about the latter, if we are to reap a harvest.

How do we encourage the seeds of kinship, love, and responsibility to send their tender roots deep into the soil of our belief and our action? How do we encourage them to reach towards the sunlight, healthy and strong?

The great mystic Teresa of Avila gives me some gardening advice:

A beginner must think of himself as of one setting out to make a garden in which the Lord is to take His delight, yet in which the soil is most unfruitful and full of weeds. His Majesty uproots the weeds and will set good plants in their stead. Let us suppose that this is already done—that a soul has resolved to practice prayer and has already begun to do so. We have now, by God's help, like good gardeners, to make these plants grow, and to water them carefully, so that they may not perish, but may produce flowers which shall send forth great fragrance to give refreshment to this Lord of ours, so that He may often come into the garden to take His pleasure and have His delight among these virtues. Let us now consider how this garden can be watered, so that we may know what we have to do....[12]

Volumes have been written on the nourishment that we can receive from the church: its scriptures, sacraments, and community life. There is a further kind of prayer nourishment, however, which we can receive from the earth through our senses. Through using those gifts God has given us—seeing, listening, smelling, touching, eating, and the movement of our bodies—we can welcome living water into our prayer and into our action, so that we can contribute our part to the fruitful harvest intended by God.

CHAPTER 8

Seeing

The artist Frederick Franck tells the story of discovering his grandfather's stereopticon. It consisted of:

twin lenses in a leather-covered housing, lined with red velvet. From this housing a kind of slide rule jutted forward, with a device at its end in which you placed twin photographs. Then, pressing the velvet edge to your face, you saw through the lenses an oak, not flat as in a picture, but all in the round, as a living presence.... And so it came about that sometimes, when getting tired on the long, lonely hikes I loved—the fields, hills and hedges began to look listless and flat in a dull two-dimensionality—I found I could order my eyes: "Now look through the stereopticon!" They would obey and the third dimension was at once restored. Every sprig of grass came to life and stood there separately in its own space; clumps of trees broke up into individual beings, each one springing from its own roots, deep in the earth.[13]

When I was eight years old, I had a similar experience when my family and teachers recognized that I was myopic. I will never forget my incredulity when I wore my glasses for the

first time during the twenty-mile drive home from the ophthal-
mologist. I had known that trees had leaves—I had seen and
touched them up close—but in the distance they had always
been a green blob, like a child's painting. Now I saw layer
upon layer of defined green shapes, a miracle of exquisite detail. When I want to remind myself of the wonder of seeing, I
remember the view from that car window years ago.

Even if you have never had occasion either to play with a
stereopticon or to experience for the first time the marvel of
corrective lenses, there are other ways to discover the ability
to focus. Perhaps you have the good fortune to know some
young children who can teach you.

Each spring, I have the privilege of introducing my tiniest
pupils to one of nature's small wonders. I bring them pussywillows, usually the first they have ever seen, for these children were only infants when pussywillows bloomed the
previous year. When I place the pussywillows in the children's
small hands, a hush falls, as tiny fingers stroke the gray fur.
Wondering eyes try to fathom the small grey object. Is it a tail?
Is it an ear? Does it purr? Will it move? Will it grow? What is it?

The bodies and minds of the children are completely absorbed in the task of *seeing* the pussywillow, of plunging into
its mystery. This kind of contemplative "seeing" is much more
than "looking"; it is an activity not just of the eyes, but of the
whole being. Children are natural contemplatives.

Long ago, we were all able to see like these children exploring the mystery of the pussywillow. The act of seeing was
something that absorbed us, body and mind, as it does my
two- and three-year-old friends. As adults, however, most of us
just glance and look away except upon those rare occasions
when something unusual catches our attention. We have forgotten our ability to see *contemplatively*, an ability that was
so natural when our hands were tiny and our eyes fresh with
wonder.

One way of focusing is to choose a particular *place* and promise ourselves to notice it every time we pass it. For the artist Claude Monet, this practice bore fruit in a series of twenty-eight paintings of the extraordinary west facade of the Gothic cathedral in Rouen, at different times of day and in different weathers. Monet shows us the cathedral emerging from the blue shadows of the morning, glowing golden in the afternoon sun, and receding into the purple dusk. We glimpse the facade through a soft mist or shield our eyes from the white, blazing sunlight of late spring. We see its silhouette against the brilliant blue winter sky or notice that the sky is turbulent with clouds. In one painting we can discern three human figures in the foreground; in another, we can almost hear the "caws" of the flock of crows scattering around one of the towers.

Whether we record the scene in oils or in the memory, such focusing can refine the art of seeing clearly. For example, the train that used to take me into New York City passes over the East River. Several years ago, I made a rule for myself: I would look up from whatever I was doing when I heard the subtle change in the clatter of the rails as the train approached the bridge. At first glance, the view was an example of urban ugliness and decay; but, as I became familiar with it, I realized that the scene from the bridge was never the same twice. The landscape of factories, vacant lots, water, traffic, and bridges taught me about the transformative power of weather and light. One day, I would behold a misty scene in which silver sky, silver water, silver buildings, and silver bridges slipped one into the other. Another day, the same landscape would be a knife-sharp etching, overarched by bright blue. Sometimes the water was dotted with seagulls; more rarely, with jagged chunks of ice. Snow turned the scene into an unlikely Christmas card. Rain turned it into a *pointillist* oil painting. Night made it glitter like Broadway. If you regularly pass a scene subject to variations in weather and light, whether it be a railroad bridge or a woodland grove or even a small windowbox garden on a neighbor's house, you can choose this technique to re-learn the art of focusing. Even a small patch of sky can suffice. Through focusing on the particular—one particular street, or grove, or window—you are, in fact, trying to see as God sees, the One for whom no fallen sparrow is insignificant.

Artists can remind us to observe the natural world around us. When we have visited Salisbury in England, I am always struck by the fact that so many visitors speak about the view of the cathedral from the southwest, across the water meadows, "just as Constable painted it." Constable has helped generations of tourists focus on that landscape; I have never heard similar praise of the lovely views from St. Ann Street or from the Bishop's Palace! Similarly, look at the drawing that begins this chapter: the perfection of a great horned owl's wing is a meditation for both artist and viewer. It will also help us remember to focus on the beauty of such a wing, should a great horned owl come our way.

Even if we do not consider ourselves artists, we can meditate through drawing, for the activity focuses our sight. We might even be surprised by the results. I remember once being a student in a drawing class where we were directed to sketch our thumb. The instructions seemed impossible: we were not to look at the paper until the task was completed. Because I conscientiously kept my gaze on the object—my thumb—rather than checking on how I was doing, the completed drawing surprised me. It actually *looked* like my thumb, and I felt like a fledgling Rembrandt!

When we learn to focus, we will discover that nature itself becomes an icon, a sacred painting drawing the observer into relationship with the reality it represents. The love blazing forth from the gaze of the Russian icon called "The Savior of the Fiery Eye" kindles embers in the soul of the observer. The Christ Child tenderly nestled against the cheek of the Theotokos (the "God-bearer"), Jesus' mother Mary, embraces the viewer with the maternal protection of God. The oak tree, along with the fish of the sea, the birds of the air, and the stars above, proclaims the glory of God and God's love for all creation, causing us to sing with the Psalmist, "O taste and see that the Lord is good!" (Ps. 34:8).

How can we learn to see with such intensity that we are not merely looking, but *tasting*?

Contemplative looking brings us into relationship with what we see. We are no longer mere spectators. In Martin Buber's words, what we gaze upon then becomes a "thou" rather than an "it." If I learn to see the world's beauty in this way, I will be unlikely to want to spoil it either through my own carelessness or through supporting in any way the powers who contribute to its destruction. If I allow myself to enjoy the world's beauty, my delight will lead me towards the Creator, whose manifold works surround me, always waiting for discovery.

Spadework

Have you ever had the experience of noticing an object, a person, or something in nature as if for the first time—perhaps even something or someone you thought you already knew well?

Many old friends who have visited our new home in Ohio remark upon an antique Pennsylvania Dutch chest in our bedroom. That chest graced our former home for twenty-eight years, but in its new setting, directly opposite the bedroom door, it is more noticeable. In similar manner, we sometimes *see* people we love as if for the first time. Absence, or the threat of illness or accident, has torn the accustomed veil from our eyes. Similar moments of clarity are important milestones in our appreciation of nature. All of us probably remember the moment we took the time to notice the intricacy of a snow-flake on our sleeve, or a maple leaf at our feet, even after years of trudging through snow and leaves.

The following exercise is best done outdoors, if the weather is fine and you can find a quiet place. Otherwise, place a natural object, such as an acorn, an egg, a seashell, a leaf, or a twig on a table before you.

Obtain a sketchpad and a soft pencil.

Sit quietly and let your eyes fall on whatever happens to be in front of you: a leaf, a blade of grass, the seashell on the table. Then close your eyes for the next five minutes.

Now open your eyes and focus on whatever you observed before: that leaf, or blade of grass, or seashell. Imagine that you and the object are alone on earth and that, in a sense, it is also looking back at you.

Take your pencil loosely in your hand. Keeping your eyes focused on the object, allow the pencil to follow on the paper what your eye is perceiving. Feel as if the point is caressing the contours of what you are gazing upon. Do not look down to check on what you are drawing; just let your hand move. Do not lift the pencil and don't worry if the pencil runs off the paper. Try to let go of any effort or self-criticism.

Take your time, and when you have finished, put your pencil down and pause a moment with eyes closed before looking at your drawing.

What have you experienced?

Frederick Franck writes, "Seeing and drawing can become one....When that happens....each leaf of grass is seen to grow from its own roots, each creature is realized to be unique, existing now/here on its voyage from birth to death. No longer do I 'look' at a leaf, but enter into direct contact with its life-process, with Life itself, with what I, too, really am."[14]

CHAPTER 9

Listening, Touching, Smelling

once descended to a crowded subway platform on Wall Street to find it had been transformed into an impromptu concert hall. The instrument was an overturned washtub to which a broom handle was attached, with a long string that was being plucked double bass fashion by a stately black street musician. At his feet was his young son, simultaneously using the washtub as a percussion section. The two of them were producing some incredibly fine jazz and the busy New Yorkers in the station were relaxed and smiling—all except for one. Firmly clamped over his ears were the headphones of a Walkman, and what he was hearing, I don't know. But he was not hearing the sounds around him which, on this rare urban occasion, were worth listening to.

How often we shut out the sounds around us! We need to refine our ability to listen, just as we refine our seeing, in order to appreciate the gift of creation. This may mean avoiding the misuse of so-called background music. Having "something going" all the time can cause us to lose our ability to listen when it is important to do so. We need to cherish silence, for silence is the environment in which true listening happens.

The late composer John Cage has written a composition scored for any instrument or combination of instruments called *4' 33"*. The performer or performers come out on stage and take their places—and then sit silently for four minutes and thirty-three seconds. They sit, and sit, and sit, and sit. What inevitably happens, after the initial discomfort, is that the audience finally begins to listen. They discover that the "silence" is alive with sounds: the rustling of programs, a few coughs, the clearing of a throat or two, perhaps a train or airplane rumbling in the distance, the shuffling of feet. John Cage's goal was to teach his audience to listen by actually programming some silence into their lives!

We do not need to buy concert tickets in order to listen to such silence, however. For the truest silence is interior: an attentive receptivity to what we hear. We need only stop our mental chatter so that we can focus on the sounds around us. As I write the first draft of this chapter on a long-distance train, I hear the following: the air-conditioning fan; the hum of conversation from other passengers; a newspaper rustling; the continuous rumble of the wheels; an irregular rattle and squeak from the connections between the cars; a child singing, and, if I listen very closely, my own breathing. The effect, when I listen to it this way, is of layers of sound, an ensemble of the "instruments" that just happen to be in a certain place at a certain time, like a spur-of-the-moment jam session.

Traveling to new places can widen our experience of sounds as well as sights. I once visited a monastery so far out in the country that the sound of a pine cone falling to the ground was like an instrumental solo, with orchestral support provided by the wind in the branches and a mocking-bird singing his heart out from the chapel tower. I also cherish in my memory the sound of the bells of Florence ringing the angelus, the bells of the cattle grazing the meadows above the little Swiss town of Wengen and adding random syncopation to the local brass band at the mountaintop café, the change-ringing of Gloucester Cathedral's great bells beckoning us to evensong. These bells help me to travel back in time. In fact, since we moved back to my old college town, the most powerful evocation of my undergraduate days has been the regular chiming of the chapel bells that mark the hour. One does not have to travel far to discover memorable listening.

When our children were small, we would occasionally go on a "sound treasure hunt" on hot summer nights. Flashlights readied, we would step outdoors into the nature's cacophony of chirps, squeaks, and trills. We chose one sound and navigated through listening. We moved silently across the lawn, past the hollyhocks, towards the rosebushes, until, half-expecting to find a monster to match the ear-splitting sawing, we quickly spotlit the singer with our flashlights. What was it? Perhaps a cricket rubbing its wings in strident song, or a tree toad. The shrillest *heldentenor* would sometimes be a creature no larger than my fingernail.

Opening our ears to nature's sounds helps us to appreciate the infinite variety of God's creation. Think about how different kinds of weather sound, from snowfall muffling the world like cotton wool to raindrops pelting the attic roof. How do different bodies of water sound—oceans, brooks, the lake's waves rippling at the shore? It does not surprise me that people seeking relief from stress often use audiotapes of environmental sounds from meadow birdsongs to ocean waves.

Our senses are a gateway to contemplation. Not only sight and hearing, but also our other senses open us to gratitude for the physical world around us.

Touch is our first sense. As a fetus grows in the womb, it feels the liquid warmth of the amniotic fluid, the pounding of the mother's heartbeat, and the gentle rocking of her body as she walks. As soon as we are born, we are held, swaddled, cradled, and rocked. And we ourselves begin touching: nursing, clutching an extended forefinger with our tiny hand, noticing when we are wet. As we explore with our hands the world outside our body, we begin to learn the difference between "I" and "other."

Touch continues to be both a comfort for us and a way of learning. I often bring into a meditation group objects that people are first asked to hold and touch. I have used everything from smooth hazelnuts and delicate seashells to small patches of different kinds of fabric cut for me from the costume collection of a friend in the theater. People always respond, "I felt calm *immediately*."

Outdoors, touch can be an adventure. When I bring in some cucumbers from the garden, my fingers tingle from the minuscule spines that protect the vegetable from predators. I invariably toss off my gardening gloves when I weed, because plunging my fingers into the soil is the only way to make sure that I am getting all the roots; then I spend several minutes looking for the gloves, the same color as the soil, at the end of the day. When I am sitting close to a patch of moss, I find that I still reach down, just as I did when I was small, to caress it. As I sit in the garden of a monastery, I watch the monks walk along the path towards the chapel, each monk reaching down *en route* to stroke Sophie, their labrador, lying in the sun like an animate holy water stoop. The world is full of texture, an entire palette of touch.

When we breathe, we cannot help using yet another sense, although we are not as gifted with it as some of earth's other creatures. I have always chuckled at glimpsing what must be the ultimate adventure in a dog's life: a trip in the family automobile with a nose out the window. What is it like, I wonder, to have a canine's sense of smell and to travel so quickly past so many fascinating scents? In our limited way, we also can breathe olfactory adventure. Notice the temperature of the air you breathe, its humidity, and its fragrances—from damp earth and honeysuckle to the manure newly dumped on the vegetable garden or farmyard, or even on the city street! Can you tell the seasons apart with your nose, from the springtime fragrant with hyacinths and lilacs to rose-scented summer to the sharp odor of autumn leaves and the bite of winter's frost? Can you breathe the scent of impending rain? Can you sniff an imminent snowstorm?

Essayist and poet Diane Ackerman says that smells "detonate softly in our memory like poignant land mines, hidden under the weedy mass of many years and experiences. Hit a tripwire of smell, and memories explode all at once."[15] The fragrance of white pine needles always transports me to the New Hampshire forest where our family spent many summers. When I smell a particular brand of incense, I hear once again the liturgy in a monastery where I once worked. Each place I have lived has its unique fragrance, from the rich smoky perfume of Paris to the farmland fragrances of Ohio.

My body is an antenna, receiving earth's messages; it helps me to open my heart to the earth and to God. Listening to the sounds and silences of the earth may well be my best way of learning to hear the voice of wisdom. Touching the exquisite variety of nature's textures helps me remember that all creation comes from God's hand. Breathing in the fragrances of the earth continues to remind me that both body and breath are the gift of my Creator.

Spadework

Put down this book and close your eyes. What do you hear? Even if you are in a quiet environment, there are sounds. It is said that John Cage once emerged from a soundproof room to declare that there was no such state as silence. He had heard the "rustling, throbbing, whooshing" of his body.[16] Is it quiet enough for you to hear your own body? What other sounds do you hear? Are there sounds coming from inside your building? Sounds from outdoors?

Take a contemplative walk in which you use each sense alone in succession. This may be done anywhere: on a city street, in a park, in your own back yard, along a country lane, in a woods, on a beach. Since western culture tends to emphasize sight to the neglect of all the other senses, leave sight for last.

Pause in your walk, close your eyes, and notice the sounds around you. Imagine that you possess only the sense of hearing. What do you hear? Are the sounds loud or soft? If you hear a repetitive sound, does it repeat in a regular rhythm or at random? Are some sounds high, some low in pitch? Can you identify them all?

As you continue walking, focus on your sense of smell. Is the air you are breathing cold or warm? Is there much humidity? Do you smell traffic fumes, a bakery, roasting chestnuts, the perfume worn by a passerby, salt water, flowers, new-mown grass, a pond?

If you can do so safely, close your eyes again and focus on the sense of touch. Don't be afraid to reach down to touch the grass or the sidewalk, or to reach up to touch the leaves on a tree. If you are in the country or a park, you can pick up a natural object, such as a twig or an acorn, and explore it with your fingers. Is it heavy or light? Smooth or rough? Can you tell its shape?

When you finally use your sense of sight during this walk, you may find that it is more focused than before.

If you can, you may even wish to include a period of focus on the sense of taste. Perhaps, when you passed that bakery, you bought a loaf of fresh bread. Or perhaps you walked near your vegetable garden, and plucked a ripe tomato!

You will find that experiencing your environment initially through the senses other than sight makes you aware of your surroundings in a new way. As you use each sense, lift up your heart in gratitude to God, who gave you so many ways to enjoy creation.

CHAPTER 10

ℰating

When I try to remember the single meal for which I have been most grateful, I keep returning to a cold Shrove Tuesday about fifteen years ago. I had spent several days on retreat at a convent about sixty miles north of my home, and I planned to return in time to observe Ash Wednesday in my own parish. That morning snow-laden clouds gathered and some flakes settled on my nose as I waited in front of the local diner for the bus that would take me back to New York, an hour and a half away. When I boarded the bus, I joined others who, like myself, were ignorant of the winter storm warnings and had set forth that day with what turned out to be unfounded optimism. Soon the snowfall became heavier, and traffic slowed. Finally, all southbound motion stopped. Through the frosted windows of the bus, we saw drivers huddled in their cars, trying to stay warm. At least we had the heat provided by our vehicle's abundant supply of gasoline.

As morning slipped into afternoon and shadows lengthened, it became quite apparent that we would never proceed even a few yards towards New York that day. However, traffic was moving in the opposite lane, albeit slowly, and when an northbound bus was spotted, four of us decided to desert our own bus, clamber over the highway divider, and flag it down.

Once aboard, I realized that my anxiety had made me oblivious to the fact that I was utterly, ravenously *hungry*. There would be, I knew, no food for at least a couple of hours, when I hoped I would be nestled into the hospitality of the convent again and invited to raid the icebox. Then a man who in my memory will always be Father Bountiful held out a hand and passed a crinkled brown paper bag along the aisle to the new passengers. It contained barely a dozen peanuts, nestled in their shells. Each of us took three. I will never forget the crackle of those three peanut shells as I broke each one in turn, nor the potent fragrance they gave forth. But especially will I remember forever the satisfaction of eating them, slowly and gratefully. They were enough to renew my energy, until in due time I did indeed raid the convent icebox.

I often wonder why I do not savor every meal as gratefully as I consumed that small offering of three peanuts. Is it because I usually take an unceasing supply of food for granted? And that reminds me of yet another story—about my younger brother Philip and a can of Reddi-Whip. Philip was four; he was devoted to chocolate pudding, and on the occasions it was served for dessert, he was allowed to decorate it with swirl upon swirl of Reddi-Whip. One day the inevitable happened: the red, white, and blue can wheezed and the Reddi-Whip ended in a feeble splutter. Philip burst into tears. We discovered that his faith in Reddi-Whip had at that moment been shattered because he was convinced the supply was eternal. It would just keep coming out of the can forever and ever. Reddi-Whip had betrayed him.

Philip, being a normal four-year-old, saw the world from the charmingly egotistical perspective of the young child. He took his food for granted, and assumed that it would continue to keep coming without end, out of the Reddi-Whip can and out of my mother's kitchen.

It is easy to smile at Philip's naiveté, but most of us are also distant from the realities of food production. We are almost as disconnected from the source of our nourishment as the child who believes that the ultimate source of his mid-morning snack of milk and cookies is the grocery store. To the child, we can explain that behind the cardboard cartons and the cellophane packages was a farmland distant from their homes, where wheat grew in fields and cows munched on grass. But how can we enlighten ourselves?

Perhaps we have to recapture the sacredness of the gift of food. I am speaking not merely of "liturgical eating," as in the eucharist, but everyday eating. A Methodist minister I know recently bought an altar at a church furnishing warehouse to use as her kitchen table. Around the border of the altar is carved, "Do this in remembrance of me." She says it will remind her that every meal is a gift from God, a sacrament in its own right.

If eating is a sacramental activity, learning to eat with attention and pleasure is a way to celebrate God's bounteous earth. That is quite obvious when food is fresh-picked from the garden. I remember, as a child, taking a salt-cellar kidnapped from the dining room table into the paradise of my grandmother's lettuce patch, where I picked the fresh green leaves, salted them, and popped them into my mouth—surely the most *nouvelle* of *nouvelles cuisines*.

The preparation of food can also become a sacramental activity, as it was for the celebrated monastery cook, Brother Lawrence, who "turned the cake frying on the pan for love of God." I know a modern-day monk who must surely pray his bread-making, to judge by the mouth-watering results. And a highly literate woman once confided to me that, when she cooked pasta and the water in the pot was just verging on the boiling point, she came close to tears because she always thought of "the spirit of God moving over the face of the waters."

Eating, like other sacred activities, draws us inexorably into relationship with the rest of creation. We do not eat in isolation, although we may eat in private, for our eating affects people and creatures far removed from our kitchens. What we eat makes a profound impact upon the land, upon our human brothers and sisters across the globe, and, of course, upon the plants and animals we consume. We may discover that we need to reconsider some of our western eating habits, particularly regarding the consumption of meat. In older cultures meat is reserved for a special celebration, as it is in the village of an African friend who wrote me about his ordination to the priesthood: "Because it was a great celebration, we killed the calf." It sounded like a version of the party at the conclusion of Jesus' parable of the Prodigal Son. While it is not the task of this book to preach about how our culture's insatiable appetite for an unending supply of such "calves" affects the earth community, I cannot help but wonder who actually enjoys a steak most: my African friend for whom it is a great celebration, or a jet-setting business executive who dines on beef every other evening. And, of course, there are increasing numbers of people who, for reasons of conscience, forego beef entirely for creative vegetarian cooking.

The earth feeds us. It is as simple as that. We cannot boast of self-sufficiency when it comes to physical nourishment. Sorcery does not work; we cannot make our food materialize out of thin air. If we choose to eat meat, we owe a debt of gratitude to the creature who gave its life for us, and we should hope that it was treated during its lifetime with the kindness we would wish for all of God's creatures. Our gratitude can extend as well to the fruits, vegetables, and grains that feed us, and to the sunshine, rain, and soil that nourished them.

Eating should be a delight, a sacrament connecting us to the earth and to the planet's community of plants and animals, not a means of estrangement from them. Eating is one of the ways

God nourishes us, through the delicately tuned network of creation.

In one of the happy coincidences of life, as I was working on this chapter, I received a letter from an effervescent friend in Paris recounting a dinner with a friend:

"I said a quick 'Thank you, God,' after tasting a particularly superb red wine. Alain said, 'I'm glad you know where all this stuff really comes from.'"

Remember, always, where this stuff really comes from.

Spadework

Do you have any special "food memories"?

We discovered that our youngest son developed quite early the ability to remember foods. The summer he was three, as we approached a mountain chairlift in New Hampshire, he exclaimed, "I remember that mountain—I had a doughnut on top of it last year!" Perhaps you remember vividly the hot oatmeal your mother cooked for you on schooldays in winter. Or can still taste the apples from your grandmother's apple tree. Or were taken to a fine restaurant on a special occasion and can taste the meal as if it were yesterday. When I was a student traveling in London, a business friend of my father took me to the Savoy Hotel, where I ordered my first smoked salmon. My parents soon thereafter received a letter assuring them I was thriving: "There is certainly nothing wrong with her appetite." Whenever I taste that delicacy now I am twenty again, at the fanciest restaurant I have ever entered.

Practice an "eating meditation." Eat a single raisin (or a piece of fresh fruit or homemade bread) very slowly. As you bite into it, notice the texture. How does it taste on different parts of the tongue? How does chewing alter the taste and the texture? How does the throat move when you are swallowing? Do not hurry, but eat with attention and enjoyment. Especially when you are hungry, such an exercise helps to nourish your grateful awareness of earth's bounty.

The next time you receive Holy Communion, remember this exercise and take time to focus, so that you truly taste the bread and the wine.

CHAPTER 11

Moving

One day I was riding my bicycle on a path along the Bronx River about twenty miles north of New York City, when a vision appeared: a snow-white heron. Braking quickly and silently, I stopped. The heron stood alert, focused on the water at its feet. From time to time, its head would dart downwards to spear an unsuspecting fish. As the bird's neck undulated in a graceful hula, the fish made the sinuous journey down to the heron's belly. I gazed at the heron until it was imprinted on my memory.

When I arrived home, I decided to play with the creative possibilities of that heron. I could write a poem about her, I could draw her on paper, or I could try to capture her grace by "drawing" the lovely curves of the heron with my hand on the blank canvas of the air. Better still, I could move like the stately bird, stepping with staccato elegance and trying to move my neck with the fluidity of a Hindu dancer.

Meditating on the heron in this way has made it possible for her to become an indelible image in my memory; I can conjure her up at will. I care passionately about her well-being, and about the well-being of her habitat. I find that I am praying, "May she always have clear water through which she peers at her dinner. May spilt oil never touch her feathers. May she always have the freedom to fly. May no one disturb her nest."

The heron is my permanent companion. I have been able to imitate her motion and thereby to step a little further into her unique world. For I, too, am one of God's animate creatures, gifted with the ability to use my body as an instrument of movement, play, and prayer.

Several years ago, my friend Lee embarked on a personal quest to discover which of the various animals in God's creation were closest to various facets of his own temperament, and to undertake the playful and prayerful task of moving like them. It was a marvel to see Lee dancing his animals.

He became the whale, plunging and breaching.

He became the deer, shy, graceful, and fleet-footed.

He became the mountain ram, stubborn and playful, charging the percussionist who accompanied the dance, side-stepping with tambour in hand.

He was the lumbering bear.

He was the great blue heron, elegant and alert.

When he danced, he became those animals. Lee communicated his love of the earth to his human audience, for whom the experience of these other species will ever after have new meaning.

Making connections with the animal world through dance is not unusual in other cultures. African or Native American dance often imitates the movement of animal species. In these traditions, dance is considered sacred. In the discipline of Tai Chi, which finds its roots in Taoism, specific movements are named for animals; raising and lowering the outspread arms while stepping delicately forward, for example, is "the stork cooling its wings." When a practitioner of Hatha Yoga, an ancient form of physical meditation from Hinduism, lies on her stomach and arches the neck and upper chest upwards, she takes the "cobra" posture.

Westerners, whose traditional dance is more removed from the natural world around us, can also use dance movement as a powerful way of reconnecting with the earth. We need not be trained dancers, for our bodies are *meant* to move. We express ourselves through our movement whether we are conscious of that fact or not.

I have taught movement classes at an Elderhostel program, where seniors, sometimes well into their seventies and eighties, have improvised their own choreography about the story of creation. Many of these men and women had never "danced" in their lives, unless it was to trace laboriously a foxtrot pattern in a social dancing class years before. My instructions were that they meditate upon an element of creation through moving like that element; it was not to be a performance, but a prayer. I can still see the powerful arms of the fit elderhosteler in his seventies slicing through the space of the chapel; he was the sun, radiance personified. Or the sea of blue chiffon scarves undulating like the ocean, held by a group of graceful grandmothers set free from inhibitions.

When I worked with a community of monks, I divided them into groups of five and gave each group a portion of the Twenty-third Psalm to interpret. One group, which was assigned the lines "He makes me lie down in green pastures and leads me beside still waters," included two of the most elderly members of the community. Everyone had expected them to be recalcitrant. We were amazed and touched when, without any prodding, they became willing shepherds, using their canes to herd the younger monks, who obediently crawled on hands and knees across the hard floor.

Why, I ask, is movement so…*moving?* Perhaps it is because it brings us close to that important frontier where playing and praying meet. Just as young children engage in "symbolic play" in order to learn about a world that is new to them, we as adults can engage in this kind of play/prayer to explore the world once again.

My first dancing lessons introduced me to the joyous possibilities of movement when I was six. My mother took me to classes held in the basement of a local church, where I was given a chiffon shift the color of a butterfly's wings. Barefoot, we moved high and low across the floor like the waves of the ocean. We swayed side to side like trees swaying in the breeze. We swirled like the wind blowing. Arms outstretched, we "flew" like butterflies. I realize now that the teacher must have been a devotee of the pioneer choreographer Isadora Duncan, who shocked the world by dancing barefoot in flowing costumes that revealed the beauty of the human body. The great Isadora often chose nature as her theme. When I danced freely with my classmates in the small world of the church basement, I was carrying on her tradition, the heritage of all those human beings who have, over the centuries, celebrated their kinship with God and with nature in the beauty of dance.

> The great sea has set me in motion.
> Set me adrift,
> And I move as a weed in the river.
>
> The arch of sky
> And mightiness of storms
> Encompasses me,
> And I am left
> Trembling with joy.[17]

Spadework

Have you ever seen dancers on television, on the stage, or in their native land who come from a culture in which dance is considered a sacred celebration of life's passages, the cycles of the year, or relationship with the divine? Have you yourself had any experience of dance? Perhaps you took creative movement classes as a child, or lessons in social dancing, tap dancing, aerobic dancing, or ballet? Do you feel free to dance, just for your own pleasure, now? If you do, how does this kind of exercise make you feel? Does it make you feel more connected to your own body, to the earth, and to God?

The "Song of Creation" is a canticle, or liturgical song, in which all aspects of creation praise God:

> O all ye works of the Lord, bless ye the Lord;
>> praise him and magnify him for ever.
> O ye angels of the Lord, bless ye the Lord;
>> praise him and magnify him for ever.

> O ye heavens, bless ye the Lord:
>> O ye waters that be above the firmament,
>>> bless ye the Lord;
> O all ye powers of the Lord, bless ye the Lord;
>> praise him and magnify him for ever.

> O ye sun and moon, bless ye the Lord;
>> O ye stars of heaven, bless ye the Lord;
> O ye showers and dew, bless ye the Lord;
>> praise him and magnify him for ever.

O ye winds of God, bless ye the Lord;
    O ye fire and heat, bless ye the Lord;
O ye winter and summer, bless ye the Lord;
    praise him and magnify him for ever.

O ye dews and frosts, bless ye the Lord;
    O ye frost and cold, bless ye the Lord;
O ye ice and snow, bless ye the Lord;
    praise him and magnify him for ever.

O ye nights and days, bless ye the Lord;
    O ye light and darkness, bless ye the Lord;
O ye lightnings and clouds, bless ye the Lord;
    praise him and magnify him for ever.

O let the earth bless the Lord;
    O ye mountains and hills, bless ye the Lord;
O all ye green things upon the earth, bless ye the Lord;
    praise him and magnify him for ever.

O ye wells, bless ye the Lord;
    O ye seas and floods, bless ye the Lord;
O ye whales and all the move in the waters,
      bless ye the Lord;
    praise him and magnify him for ever.

O ye fowls of the air, bless ye the Lord;
    O all ye beasts and cattle, bless ye the Lord;
O ye children of men, bless ye the Lord;
    praise him and magnify him for ever.

Use this text for your own meditation-through-dance, inter-
preting each image through your movements. You can do this

in a very simple manner; there is no "right" or "wrong." It is your *own* prayer, not a performance!

You can, for example, create a movement just for the refrain "Praise him and magnify him for ever." It can become a movement "mantra"—a phrase that is a repetitive prayer. Perhaps you will express the phrase through clapping your hands on "Praise him" and then let the momentum open your hands in an arc. Or the phrase may be expressed in a simple bow, or in lifting the arms to the sky. It is important to discover how *your* body wishes to express the phrase, rather than to copy someone else's ideas.

Then imagine yourself as one of those aspects of creation enumerated in the canticle. For example, when you "bless the Lord" as one of the "green things upon the earth," you might grow from a curled position on the floor and unfold like a leaf until you reach up toward the sky, or you might reach down to touch imaginary blades of grass at your feet. When you are the lightning, you can slice the air with your arms; when you are the wind, you can swirl across the space. Enjoy moving like the whales, the fowls of the air, the beasts and the cattle, as each, in turn, blesses the Lord who made them.

If you can find a musical setting of the canticle, the music will inspire and support your movement. You can also use pure instrumental music. It is interesting to move this prayer first to something like Bach chamber music, and then to some indigenous music from a non-European culture like Africa. In addition to using meditation-through-dance in solitary prayer, this is a wonderful exercise to do with others.

IV.

Compost

We have three compost heaps, and even they are not capacious enough to contain all the castoffs of our garden and our kitchen. When the leaves begin to fall, we will have to begin a new pile near the border of our small woods. Our compost piles include a variety of vegetable material: carrot peelings, strawberry hulls, tomato prunings, the weeds I have dug before they have gone to seed, grass-clippings, coffee grounds, eggshells, corn husks, dry leaves, melon rinds. Although some people might consider the contents of our piles to be "garbage," this material is not garbage. As it decays, assisted by earthworms as well as by organisms I cannot even see, my compost becomes "black gold," rich humus that will contribute to the garden's future well-being.

Composting teaches me that nothing in life is, in fact, "garbage." The way of nature is the way of use and re-use. When this lunchtime's carrot peeling is dumped on top of the seething compost pile, it enters into the slow process of becoming fertilizer for next summer's crop of carrots.

I learn, from observing nature's economy, that God intends me also to use all that I am given. I am meant to use my gifts and skills, my sorrows, and all the random happenings of life, spreading them out, as it were, in the fresh air of God to be transformed so that they can become life-giving, both for myself and for the world around me.

ifts

everal summers ago, my husband and I spent two weeks in Aspen, Colorado, a town nestled in the midst of some of the most spectacular scenery we have ever seen. A friend told us about Stuart Mace and his "Philosophy of a Green World" nature walk, and so one day we drove up Castle Creek Valley above Aspen and, with about fifteen other pilgrims, gathered in front of the cabin that served both as art gallery and home. According to instructions, we had brought a rucksack lunch and a "buoyant spirit of inquiry." Stuart Mace's brochure had described how we would spend our six hours together: "We hobnob with the myriad life in streams, ledges, meadows, forests, beaver bogs, alpine circs and springs. There is some of the 'what's-the-name?' but, mostly, 'what's the connection'? We search for the peace that comes with understanding."

Stuart Mace did not disappoint us. Leaning against an aspen tree, he began by helping us understand the valley's history. We saw in our imaginations the beauty of the original wilderness, then the busy silvermining town whose weathered remnants still stood nearby as ghostly reminders. We saw the miners departing and cattle-ranchers inheriting the fields and their cattle grazing the meadows bare. What Stuart found here almost fifty years ago, when he entered the valley's history as naturalist and caretaker, was a depleted ecosystem gasping for life.

For purposes of healing the damage wrought by mining and grazing, Stuart could have consulted the scores of books available on mountain ecology. Or, if he had been impatient, he could have skipped the books and chosen action instead: he could have hauled topsoil up the steep mountain roads and then scattered fistfuls of wildflower seeds in order to work an impressive miracle.

Stuart did neither. Instead, he decided to become a patient observer: nature's pupil. He spent his days roaming the mountain valley's streams, fields, and woodlands. He observed that each species of plant thrived in the particular environment that was most congenial: sage in the dry spots, wild parsley in the damp places, columbine in the mottled shade of the aspen groves, sunflowers and Indian paintbrush in the hot sun.

Stuart watched and waited. Each year, more seeds were wafted to the valley. Some found their places; some did not. Each summer more plants flourished; in autumn their greenery withered and their seeds scattered.

It took a long time. Some plants, he told us, waited twenty years for proper weather for blooming. Slowly but surely, nature gave the gift of new life, and in the end, the valley was once again healthy: sage was in the dry spots, wild parsley in the damp places, columbine in the mottled shade of the aspen groves, and sunflowers and Indian paintbrush in the hot sun. Stuart did not need to convince us that nature's harmony had been restored; we needed only to look around us at the bright profusion of flowers.

We set out to walk carefully behind Stuart, trying not to tread on any of the subject matter under discussion as Stuart talked. Observing nature as we were doing, he said, is an "outward meditation, with your inner stops all open and your mouth shut." When we do this, we hear nature speaking to us of "harmony, balance, empathy, humility, frugality, and gentleness." Nature had taught him that life is a gift, a banquet at which we are all guests.

In the natural world, nothing is ever given that is not returned. The sun is the great gift-giver, providing the green plants with energy to produce leaves, stems, blossoms, and seeds. These plants fulfil their destiny, in turn, as gift-givers, providing food for earth's other creatures as well as delight for our eyes. Even when they die, they give. Lying on the forest floor or in the windswept meadow, they gradually decay, returning the sun's gift of energy to the soil so that it can be used by succeeding generations. Plants do not know about theft or hoarding, nor about garbage.

What I have come to call "Stuart's Meadow" has become a permanent image of harmony for me. When I try to visualize a place of peace and beauty, I find myself once again standing in an aspen grove looking at a field full of wildflowers and hearing Stuart's soft voice open the book of nature's wisdom to us.

I learn many things from this meadow, including the need to respect my own gifts and skills—*my* gifts, not the ones I've been told I should have by voices either within me or outside me. In a sense, nature "prays" by being absolutely true to itself: "Glorify the Lord, all ye works of the Lord!" The aspen tree glorifies God by being an aspen, not by trying to be a sunflower. I also can glorify God by remaining true to myself.

Then the meadow reminds me that I am to use the gifts rather than to keep them to myself. When I try to visualize myself as a meadow, I may discover some reasons why I have failed to use my gifts. I may discover that my sagebrush is trying valiantly to grow in the damp shade of the aspens. My "sagebrush" might be my capacity for seeing things in a new and fresh way, and perhaps I have kept that in the shade because of shyness or cowardice, instead of speaking out prophetically and courageously. Maybe I have to step out from under the shadows cast by timidity so that I will be free to grow. Perhaps, on the other hand, my columbines are wilting in the scorching sun. My "columbines" might be a gift for reflection and prayer, needing protection from the heat of overactivity, so that they can contribute both to my own health and that of the community.

The health of Stuart's mountain valley is derived from the community life of the its animals and plants. The columbines need the shade of the aspens, just as the sage needs the sun, and each is a part of a great network of interdependence. I need to understand that using my gifts is important not just for my own health, but that of the communities to which I belong—the family, the town, the nation, the world.

Perhaps I am sagebrush and columbine. Perhaps you are aspen and sunflowers, or Indian paintbrush. I had been thinking of Stuart Mace as a modern Thoreau, but perhaps he really was a contemporary St. Paul, who might have written in this fashion to present-day Corinthians:

"Just as the valley is one valley and has many flowers, and all the flowers of the valley, though many, are part of this valley, so it is with the community of earth....Indeed, the valley does not consist of one flower but of many. If the wild parsley would say, 'Because I am not a columbine, I do not belong to the valley,' that would not make it any less a part of the valley. If the whole valley were aspen trees, where would the meadow be? If the whole valley were Indian paintbrush, where would the forest shade be? But God has so arranged the valley that there be no dissension within it. If one suffers, all suffer; if one thrives, all rejoice. Now the community of the earth is the mountain valley of Christ, and individually you are the flowers."

Spadework

What place on earth would you choose if you were asked to visualize a scene in nature that has impressed you with a sense of its harmony and health? What has contributed to that sense? Is there a variety of plant and animal species? Do they depend upon one another? Can you understand the scene as a microcosm of what the entire earth community should be?

When I try to choose my favorite spot, I often think of Sissinghurst, a garden in England. Sissinghurst is an example of the interplay of human endeavor and nature. Garden-spaces open one into the other like a series of chapels, each with its own palette of colors: a white garden, a purple border, a garden of herbs, a cottage garden glowing with the colors of sunset. Roses and clematis clamber up weathered brick walls and ramble through the rose garden. Sissinghurst hums with the music of bees, birds, and gardeners happily comparing notes; roses and jasmine perfume the soft air of the Kentish countryside. There is a sense of harmony and peace in this place, both the gift of God and the work of human hands.

Take some time to relax and center, focusing on your breathing. Now ask yourself the question, "What are the activities or occupations that make me feel happiest or most fulfilled?" This question may seem egotistical, but it is based on the fact that we tend to do best what we love best. Your own sense of harmony, health, and happiness may be a clue in discovering your natural gifts. Perhaps you lose yourself when you are engaged in teaching someone, and then realize that you have really *found* your true self. Perhaps you spend every available moment in your home workshop doing carpentry.

Perhaps you feel your whole self stretching and growing when you volunteer in a hospital, or when you participate in a dance class.

You may find it useful to write down this list of gifts. These are God's gifts to you. They are valuable; God does not create "junk." Using them is like the green plant using the gift-energy of the sun. Spend some time in silence, holding these gifts before God and thanking God for them.

Then visualize your own "mountain valley." What is the context in which you live and work? With what people? Spend some time mentally picturing your day-to-day surroundings. Now ask yourself, "What are some of the ways my gifts could best flourish, given the context in which I live? How can I use what God has given me?" This question helps us to be realistic and creative in the use of our gifts.

Do not be anxious about achieving any immediate results with this exercise. Remember that some plants took twenty years to blossom in Stuart's meadow! The important thing is a change in attitude about what you have to offer and your willingness to offer it.

Sorrows

When we become disciples of nature, we learn that we are both growing and dying at every moment. We learn that change is as integral to the human condition as it is to the mountain valley or the sandy seashore. Nothing, absolutely nothing, is constant except the overarching love of the God who created this ever-changing universe.

I once had a colleague whose home contained an impressive array of house plants. Looking at the array of healthy green foliage, I asked her to share her secret. "My secret?" she responded. "When they begin to die, I throw them on the compost heap."

Throwing away plants—whether they be houseplants at the end of their lives or vegetable seedlings at the beginning of theirs—onto the compost heap is extremely difficult for me. The back of the carrot seed package directs me to "scatter seed in the row at the rate of three to five seeds per inch." Then come those awful words: "When seedlings have three leaves, *thin* to stand two inches apart." I usually cannot bring myself to follow the directions to the letter. I cheat, hoping that they will grow equally well if they are only one-and-a-half inches from their neighbors.

I want to hold on the houseplants and to each carrot seed-
ling. I need, instead, to learn that their dying is a way of giving. Their dying contributes to living.

On our nature walk, Stuart Mace explained that death is the
keystone of nature's life-cycle. If deciduous trees stubbornly
clung to their leaves, there would be no black loam at their
roots to nurture next year's greenery. Giving is the pattern in
the animal world as well, although it might also be seen as taking, depending on one's place in the chain! Algae give their
lives in the fish's watery cafeteria, who in turn meet their end
when a sharp-eyed seagull plunges to spear them. Each death
gives life to something else. The things of the earth give themselves for one another and for future generations.

Receiving, and then giving back, is the way nature works.
Since we are part of God's earthly creation, we share in its cy-
cles of living and dying. "To My Old Brown Earth," a song by
Pete Seeger, expresses it well:

> To my old brown earth,
> And to my old blue sky
> I now give these last few molecules of "I";
> And you who sing and you who stand nearby,
> I do charge you not to cry.
> Guard well our human chain;
> Watch well you keep it strong
> As long as sun will shine;
> And this our home
> Keep pure and sweet and green,
> For now I'm yours
> And you are also mine.

I find Seeger's song strangely comforting in the midst of the
denial of death that surrounds me in this culture. Knowing
that we will ultimately give back our physical selves—"these
last few molecules of I"—to the earth, we can choose to live

with either gloom or *humor*, which is delightfully related to the word "humus," the Latin form of *adamah*.

A teacher even wiser than Stuart Mace once spoke the language of the mountain valley: "Those who find their life will lose it, and those who lose their life for my sake will find it" (Matthew 10:39). When I have learned that truth, I can apply it elsewhere, letting die what needs to die. Perhaps I can even learn to welcome change, or at least to make peace with it. Most of it I cannot control, after all. Our bodies shed dead cells, and new ones take their place. One kind of family life— life with young children—dies, so that it can grow into another kind of family life in which young adults and their parents discover a new mutuality. Our work changes, our friendships change, we move, we age, we lose dear ones. All of the dying is the compost of our lives, even as we resist it. It is, in the end, the way we live.

In the Japanese tradition of *ikebana*, flower-arranging is considered a form of meditation. A friend of mine who practices *ikebana* tells me that change is of the essence of her arrangements. At the moment she finishes the *ikebana*, the arrangement begins its process of decay. The passage towards decay is considered an aspect of its beauty, an attitude that those of us who are aging (namely, everyone) in our youth-oriented culture can envy.

Nature teaches me to let go of past sorrows or resentments so that I can move on. It is an environmental issue: if my inner landscape is polluted with hoarded resentments and sadness, I cannot see beyond myself to the world around me. Infertile lives beget infertile meadows, woodlands, or communities. When I allow myself to let go, I am often surprised by the power of healing, as gratuitous and surprising as the sun bursting through clouds on a dull day.

Like the plants in the mountain meadow, we are dying and growing all the time. Every event of life, no matter how tragic, can become a means of growth for us; it depends on what we do with it. There is no garbage—only compost.

When we recognize the rhythm of receiving and giving, living and dying, as God's intention for our world, we will be more reluctant to create garbage, and more imaginative in dreaming up ways to use and reuse every part of God's creation that comes our way, ourselves included.

Spadework

Take some time to reflect on a sorrowful event in your life.

Have you discovered that, in order to move beyond it, you must first accept it as part of life along with the feelings it arouses? Do you have any ideas about how you can use this negative event so that it will be part of the richness of life?

As you think about this sorrow, you may discover that it has already contributed to life's richness. Perhaps a difficult work situation taught you things about human nature or about yourself that you would not have otherwise learned. Perhaps, after a tragic loss, you became part of a community of others with a similar loss and discovered through it your ability to help others.

Take a meditative walk in a natural area—some woods, a park, a wild meadow—or spend some prayer time in a garden. Take special note, as you look about you, of the stages of nature's cycle of living and dying. Is anything just beginning to grow? Perhaps there is a tender green shoot on a plant, or a leaf just now unfurling. Is there anything in full blossom or full leaf? Can you see any seed pods beginning to form? Are leaves beginning to turn yellow? What is on the ground? Are there decaying leaves from the previous year? When you dig down a little with your fingers, do you find some of them decaying into rich humus? Do you notice the interplay of life and death?

Observe the cycles of your houseplants in the same way. Notice new buds and new leaves. Watch them as they mature. When leaves or blossoms wither and drop, instead of throwing them in the garbage, cut them up with scissors and put them in a small plastic garbage bag. Add a small amount of water and, if you wish, a bit of compost starter, available from nurseries. You may add vegetable trimmings, like carrot, apple or potato peelings cut into small pieces. Keep the mixture damp, and shake and turn it from time to time. Eventually you will have good rich humus to use in fertilizing your plants or potting new ones.

Reflect upon your own acceptance of the cycles of nature. Think about the goodness of the process. Ask God to help you appreciate this cycle of living and dying, and your own place in it.

CHAPTER 14

Weather

There is one element of gardening, above all, which is absolutely unpredictable: the weather. We have no control over it. It makes our attempt to grow a garden an ongoing drama in which the weather sometimes collaborates with our efforts and sometimes sabotages them.

There was a drought the summer we moved to Ohio. The earth was cracked and hard, lawns were parched, and passing a cornfield or a vegetable garden could not help but arouse compassion. We planted a token garden, took off for a month's vacation, and returned to find that half our plants had withered despite the neighbors' solicitous care. They said the sun had beaten down, day after day after day, with no respite. To add insult to injury, it had rained twice in the next town; to get there, the storm clouds had sailed over our neighborhood, oblivious to its parched state.

The next spring, we installed an irrigation system. It consisted of two hundred and fifty feet of hose made from recycled rubber tires, with a water regulator that was supposed to be attached to the faucet. After planning the perennial bed, I snaked the hose in a pattern that would guarantee a good supply of water for every plant and then buried the black rubber under an inch of soil. I was ready.

That summer, it poured. Water stood two inches high at the edge of each flower bed and in the aisles of the vegetable garden. Rain beat down the petunias, the tomatoes, and the cucumber vine. Rain beat against windows. Rain rose in basements. Rain ruined picnics. The only time I used the irrigation system it rained the next day.

I had equally meager control over the fate of some winter rye we had planted in the fall. The rye was meant to grow in the autumn, protect the garden from erosion over the winter, and feed the soil with nitrogen in the spring when it was turned under. In February, the weather turned as warm as May, and, taking the cue, the rye reached for the sky. By mid-March, it was several feet tall. What we didn't bargain for was spring rain, and the fact that the rye would prevent the soil from drying out until the beginning of June. Our nitrogen project caused us to the be last people in town to get our garden in.

A Christmas cactus, which I had tended successfully for several years, always flourished when it spent the summer outdoors. When I brought the other houseplants indoors in the autumn, I would leave the cactus behind on the patio for a week or two, since a few cool evenings would help it set its buds. I didn't bargain for an early frost one night. The next morning, the leaves looked like cooked spinach.

There is very little one can do to prevent the weather's ravages, except watering during a drought or protecting tender plants when a frost is predicted. Someday, perhaps someone will figure out how to *dry out* a garden, but it hasn't happened yet. Usually, when the weather doesn't suit, all one can do is wait for a better time.

We have friends who lived for a while in a state noted for the constancy of its fine weather. They couldn't stand it. They told us that they were always so *comfortable* that they were bored. So they moved to mercurial New York, where the saying is, "If you don't like the weather, wait an hour."

Changeable weather is but one aspect of the apparent chaos that scientists tell us is fundamental to the the functioning of the universe. That is as true in theology as in physics:

> We are face-to-face with a fundamental change in our view of creation, triggered by new understandings across the scientific specturm. A natural order which seemed as predicable as Newton's laws has been re-placed by one full of "the heresy of chance." Freedom, turbulence, and chaos surround us, and we are here to open our minds to these new discoveries.[18]

I know about freedom, turbulence, and chaos from the weather that bakes, freezes, dries, or drenches our garden. And I also know it from other weather patterns over which I have no control, the patterns of life that seem to swirl all around me. They can come in the form of illness, accidents, or aging. They can be financial problems, stressful professional situations, or family crises. They can be caused by those vio-lent natural disasters that are mislabeled "acts of God," such as tornados or earthquakes.

These periods may parch us with drought, and we may be-lieve ourselves to be "in a dry and weary land where there is no water" (Ps. 63). Or they may inundate us like a torrential rain, so that we feel we are sinking "in deep mire, where there is no foothold" (Ps. 69). They may sear like a heat wave, freeze like a blizzard, or buffet us like the winds of a hurricane.

Physicists suggest that randomness, or chaos, creates a place of opportunity. If everything was predictable, nothing new would be likely to occur. Chaos helps make possible new connections between things.

When the weather surprises me, drenching or drying up the garden, I wait and I watch. Perhaps the weather will change. Perhaps I will gather courage from knowing we all are sharing the same weather. Perhaps I can do something about it, like protecting the lettuce seedlings. Perhaps I will need to consider some changes in the garden.

When life's chaos surprises me, I wait and I watch as well. I try to hear the message of Reinhold Niebuhr's prayer: "God, grant us grace to accept with serenity the things that cannot be changed, courage to change the things that should be changed, and the wisdom to distinguish the one from the other."[19] I gather courage from knowing that changeable weather is part of the human condition. I find support in my connections with other people and look for new opportunities to arise out of the turbulence.

Above all, I try to remember my dependence on the One in whom there is "no variableness, neither shadow of turning." I think of St. Teresa of Avila, braving the storms of her fanatic era and traipsing around arid Spain in her mission to weed out corruption and establish a reformed Order of Carmelites. She endured, in Phyllis McGinley's words, "floods, cold, heat, lack of provisions, and unspeakable country inns with the hardihood of an old soldier. 'God gives us much to suffer for Him,' Teresa wrote, 'if only from fleas, ghosts, and bad roads.'"[20] One would not expect that such a beleagured soul would contribute her own "serenity prayer" to Christian literature:

> Let nothing perturb you, nothing frighten you.
> All things pass;
> God does not change.
> Patience achieves everything.
> Whoever has God lacks nothing.
> God alone suffices.[21]

Teresa's irrepresible joy stemmed from her discovery that God was found, constant and caring, at the still center of every storm. Remembering that "God alone suffices" helps me to get on with my life and my prayer, no matter what the weather.

Spadework

Can you think of times in your life when you were in a difficult situation that was beyond your control? How did you respond?

One of my friends speaks of the total helplessness he felt at the moment he was wheeled into the operating room for surgery. What he really wanted to do was to shout, "Stop! I don't want to do this." But he made himself relax, put himself in God's hands, and the next thing he knew he was in the recovery room.

One of the stories my mother-in-law used to tell was about sitting on her front porch and seeing a tornado carry away the church in which she was to be married the following month. In her case, the reponse was obvious: the wedding was held in another church!

Make a point of noticing the weather every day for the period of a week. Set aside about fifteen minutes each day for a period of meditation, and ask yourself these questions:

Is it sunny or cloudy?

What color is the sky?

How does the air feel? Dry, or humid? Balmy, or cool?

Is there any wind? How does the wind affect the trees?

Is it raining, or has it been raining? Snowing?

How has the weather affected the grass, the garden, or the street?

How does the weather affect *me*? Does it depress me or fatigue me? If I were outdoors, would it make me feel uncomfortable? Or would it energize and invigorate me?

How does the weather affect other people? Is it possible that weather *I* don't like is exactly the kind of weather that someone else is wishing for?

How do I feel about the fact that I cannot control the weather?

Are there parallels between the way I observe and react to the weather, and the way I observe and react to the things in life that I cannot control? Am I able to depend on God's strength and solace in these situations?

V.

Pests

Our garden is no carefree Eden. Hordes of insects, innumerable weeds, and a large brown rabbit compete with us for our garden's produce. No matter how vigorous the plants, some form of pest control is necessary.

The brown rabbit got there first, before we put up the fence. We had planted six green broccoli seedlings and left for the weekend. When we returned, there were two broccoli seedlings. The following day, there were none. That afternoon, we headed for a farm supply store to buy chicken-wire. With a rabbit, a barrier is the best answer.

We have handled other competitors in a variety of ways. For the insects, one possibility would have been a holocaust: zapping those who were eating the garden, as well as the insects who ate *them*, with insecticide. Since that made little sense, we chose other methods. We planted marigolds: their yellow blooms take away insect appetites, in the meantime improving the view by punctuating the green of the vegetables. If the insects persist, we either agree to share our bounty with them or we spray the plants with soapy water. As for weeds, they are best pulled up, unless a mulch has prevented their growth in the first place. Pest control takes some effort.

Effort is needed, too, in the cultivation of our lives. We live in a world in which good and evil are subtly intermingled within ourselves as well as in the world outside. We must recognize those things that eat up, dry out, inhibit, poison, or consume the fulfillment of God's purpose for us. Once we have recognized them, we can then choose appropriate means of "pest control."

It is clear, as we look at those ills that face us as we move into the twenty-first century, that the seven deadly sins of pride, envy, anger, covetousness, gluttony, lust, and sloth are not remnants of the past, but alive and well. They may go under different names—self-righteousness, greed, burnout, depression, despair—but they still choke our growth and consume our resources. It is also clear that their antidote continues to be, not surprisingly, God's gift of the virtues of love, hope, and faith.

CHAPTER 15

Emptiness and Greed

four-year-old Kate was accustomed to bringing a beloved security blanket to the weekly class in which we learned about God and the world through story, music, and dance. Our sessions always include a few minutes when we sit together on a large picnic blanket while I tell the story that will be the day's theme. One day, as I began to spread out my blanket, Kate quickly spread out her small blanket beside it and motioned that we were to sit on hers instead of mine.

Surprised but obedient, all eight of us squeezed onto Kate's blanket and I began: "Once some people tried to bring a sick friend to Jesus. They carried him to the house where he was healing people, but they could not get in the door...." A tug on the blanket. And another. Kate had changed her mind. She tugged persistently and silently until finally we all scrambled to our feet. Kate gathered her beloved object into her arms and held it close. Finally she spoke: "Do you know why I had to take my blankie back?" "No, Kate, why?" "Because I love it so much."

Whenever I tell that story, I know that I am telling it not just about Kate but about myself. It is a story about all of us, because it so graphically illustrates the human condition. Kate couldn't decide: should she spread out her wealth, or should she keep it to herself? Should she be free, or should she be afraid? We are equally ambivalent as we confront, again and again, the question of whether our lives will be marked by giving or by greed, by love or by fear.

The emptiness that is part of the human condition makes us desirous creatures. Empty lungs gasp for oxygen and empty stomachs rumble for food in order to draw our attention to their need. Empty hearts and empty spirits long for God, who alone will satisfy them.

We are needy, and we usually know that our neediness cannot be met by the things we mistakenly clasp to ourselves. We keep hearing the seductive voices nevertheless, voices urging us to look for eternal satisfaction in the things of this world.

Doris Janzen Longacre writes about an American who visited the People's Republic of China. The American was aghast at what he considered to be brainwashing. How could people tolerate the constant barrage of slogans telling everybody what to think? Then, suddenly he came to the realization that American commercial interests are the equal of any totalitarian political poster or radio propaganda, conveying "nonstop messages just as inane."[22]

These messages are more subtle, and therefore even more insidious, than any political propaganda. If I feel empty of love, the ads tell me, I can be alluring by purchasing the parfumeur's latest creation. If I feel empty of beauty, I can buy a designer tee shirt or couturier cocktail dress. If I feel empty of friendship, I can join other laughing companions imbibing a particular brand of something fizzy. If I feel empty of worth, I can fill myself with importance by making my bank account grow. If I feel empty of power, I can drive a fast sports car. If I feel empty of excitement, I can sail on a world cruise.

All these things do give pleasure. I am the first to confess that I would enjoy dressing in something nice and spraying on a dash of fragrance in order to sip champagne or Perrier on ice at the home of a friend, knowing all the time I had enough cash in my wallet for carfare home—even, perhaps, for a car—and plenty to spare. Such pleasures are, indeed, one of the gifts of the Creator. In my heart of hearts, however, I know that these are not permanent sources of happiness.

We can either learn to live with our innate emptiness and let it draw us towards God, or we can permit it to turn into greed. When it does the latter, it breeds the overconsumption that creates such terrible patterns of injustice and misery for the world's poor, as well as environmental destruction. It seems to me that an economy based on the encouragement of consumption cannot work in the long run; it is bound to fail because it is, ultimately, so unsatisfying. That is because human nature is so designed that we can never get enough. Our desire is infinite because it is meant to draw us to God. It cannot be quenched by wealth, or designer clothing, or alcohol, or any of the myriad other security blankets to which we tend to clutch. Our infinite desire for finite things makes us, the planet's wealthiest citizenry, some of the neediest.

My friend Carol, a Maryknoll sister, worked for several years with the indigenous people of the Panamanian jungle. She taught in several small villages more than a day's journey on foot from any town. The people live a simple life in conditions we would be likely to describe as poverty. But Carol tells me that there is no word for "poor" in the peasant's native language! They share what they have with one another, and their needs are satisfied.

Carol is based in Chicago now and drives to parishes all over the midwest to spread the word about Maryknoll's mission in Panama. When she visited us recently, she spoke of her years in the jungle with nostalgia—"At night, you can see every star in the sky"—and I found my own longing for a simpler life reinforced. Perhaps a similar longing on the part of the general public, dissatisfied with today's materialism, is responsible for the popularity of a song from the Shaker tradition:

'Tis the gift to be simple, 'tis the gift to be free,
'tis the gift to come down where we ought to be,
and when we find ourselves in the place just right,
'twill be in the valley of love and delight.
When true simplicity is gained
to bow and to bend we shan't be ashamed;
to turn, turn, will be our delight
'til by turning, turning we come round right.

This text reverberates with the freedom and joy of an approach to life based on "living lightly on the earth" instead of acquiring and hoarding. Since the Shakers knew that the pleasures and comforts of the earth were God's gift to them, they used them with gratitude and imagination for the good of the entire community. When we live like that, the song assures us, we will find ourselves "where we ought to be"—a place of true *humility* and *humanity*, love and delight. As we bow and bend to the realities of living, we join with all creation, circling and turning in a light-hearted dance.

This song could be considered a choreographic interpretation of the abundant life preached by a penniless itinerant preacher almost two thousand years ago. It is the kind of abundant life that does not deplete the abundant life of other creatures, nor the air, water, or land of this planet. Instead, it contributes to the health of all. When I recently looked at the passage in the fifth chapter of Matthew's gospel known as the Beatitudes," I realized it would be an excellent candidate for yet one more environmental action list of "Nine Ways to Save the Earth."

"Blessed are the poor in spirit," Jesus said, describing those who depend on God rather than on material possessions for their joy. Blessed are those who mourn, for they have compassion for the world's pain. Blessed are the meek, who recognize, in all humility, their own origins in *humus*, in *adamah*. Blessed are those who hunger and thirst for righteousness, for they will follow the call to courageous love-in-action. Blessed are the merciful, for they will reach out kind hands to the entire creation. Blessed are the pure in heart, whose lives are a clear reflection of God's love. Blessed are the peacemakers who beckon others to the valley of love and delight. Blessed are you when people revile you and persecute you and utter all kinds of evil against you on my account, for this way of life, you will find, involves going against the grain of society—but it is the only way to joy.

The Beatitudes, or "blessings," live up to their name, for they might well be considered a recipe for filling our emptiness with lasting happiness. The major ingredient is sharing: sharing our love, ourselves, and our resources. It takes a lifetime of learning, but we can, like Kate, begin small. Soon we will realize that we have found ourselves by letting go of what we had once thought was dreadfully important, and that we are finally dancing in the valley of love and delight.

Spadework

Can you relate to the story of Kate and her blanket? Do you have "loves" that you want to clutch to yourself—such as love of security, praise, or material possessions—and that get in the way of a deeper, more universal desire for the whole creation's well-being?

The theologian Dorothee Soelle, writing in *Christianity and Crisis*, identifies five "responses on seeing a flower":

> Ah!
> Oh, beautiful—I want it, but I will let it be!
> Oh, beautiful—I want it, I will take it!
> Oh, beautiful—I can sell it!
> So?[23]

Does this suggest what acquisitiveness does to our pleasure in gifts we are all meant to share?

Have a pencil and paper handy. Take some time to relax your body and center your mind. Then focus prayerfully on this question: "What is most important to me in life?"

Begin writing down your thoughts. Perhaps your list will read, "My family. Baseball. My garden." Perhaps your list will read, "Having free time. Working in a room with a window. Living in a harmonious atmosphere." Perhaps it will read, "Listening to music. Keeping my health. My relationship with God."

Keep this list so that you can reflect on it and add to it in the future. How honest have you been with yourself?

Which things on the list are things you can have by giving or sharing? Which are things you can have through self-discipline? Which are things you need to buy?

Do you really arrange your life so that you give time to the most important things, or do you merely give lip service to them?

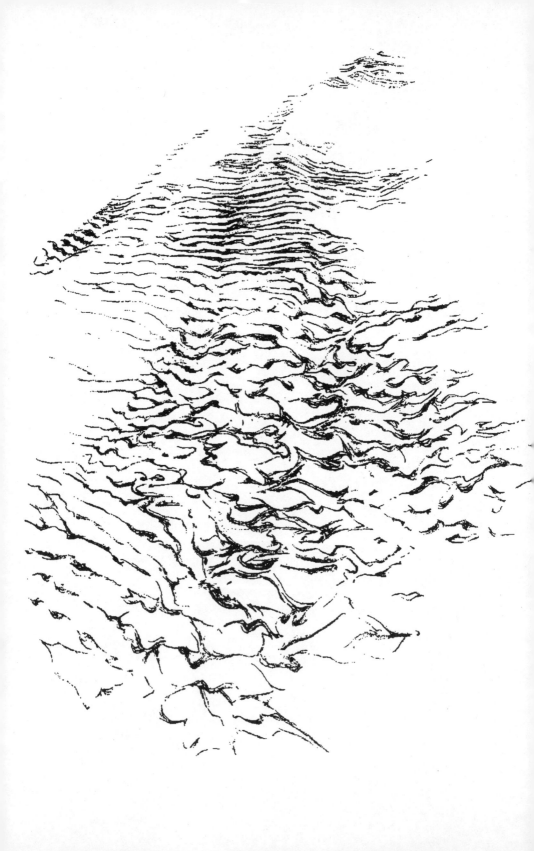

CHAPTER 16

Self-Righteousness and Guilt

There is a poem by C. P. Cavafy called "Waiting for the Barbarians," set in ancient Rome, that begins, "What are we waiting for, assembled in the forum? The barbarians are due here today." As the poem proceeds, it appears that the entire life of the city is based on the expected arrival of the barbarians, the "bad guys." Meanwhile, the fabric of society is coming unravelled: the senate has adjourned, the emperor sits waiting at the city gate; and the orators no longer make speeches. It is all the fault of the approaching hordes.

The poem concludes:

Why this sudden bewilderment, this confusion?
(How serious people's faces have become.)
Why are the streets and squares emptying so rapidly,
everyone going home lost in thought?

Because night has fallen
and the barbarians haven't come.

And some of our men just in from the border say
there are no barbarians any longer.

Now what's going to happen to us without barbarians?
Those people were a kind of solution.[24]

There are two attitudes towards guilt that can eat away at meaningful action and authentic prayer on behalf of the earth, and "Waiting for the Barbarians" gives a witty illustration of one of them. It is the way of casting all the blame onto others. Our anger rages at the "barbarians" in multinational corporations who market infant formula to lactating mothers, at greedy poachers stalking wild elephants for their ivory tusks, at the careless rich who live in luxury beside their homeless neighbors huddling for warmth on sidewalk grates. We scold other nations for harpooning whales, other states for causing acid rain, other towns for dumping toxic waste, other people for unethical consumer habits. Some of the blame may indeed lie in these places, and we can try to effect change through letter-writing, boycotts, and responsible voting. But if our activity consists only in casting blame while feeling smug ourselves, it misses the mark.

The fact is that we are all part of the problem, and these "barbarians" are a means to avoid looking at our own guilt. We *all* carry within us the capacity to spoil our earth. Our egocentricity, like our emptiness, is part of the human condition. We struggle with our desire to be gods, the lords of creation. That is what the Genesis tale of Adam, Eve, and the apple is about: our grasping at power. Sometime in pre-history, when we "fed" collectively on the apple of Eden, we fell into possibility: the possibility of using our new potential for healing, or for destruction. We have used our inventiveness to build hospitals, and we have used it to build nuclear missile silos. We have used our power to convince shareholders that bulldozing the rainforest is the only way to ensure a constant supply of food for our tables, or we have used it in lobbying for a wetlands protection law in the state legislature. We can go either way. That is true for the human race, and true for us each as individuals. Just by living in a modern industrialized country, we have aided and abetted the work both of building and of destroying.

The editors of *Earth Prayers* put it this way:

> While many of us are aware of the destruction taking place on our planet, it is difficult to integrate this knowledge into our daily life. What do we do when it is not war that is killing us, but progress? When the problem is not the actions of an evil "other," but ourselves? We fear the despair such information provokes. We don't want to feel the grief over all that is lost, nor our own complicity in the damage. This denial of feeling takes a heavy toll on us, impoverishing our sensory and emotional life. Ultimately, it puts us out of touch with reality.[25]

There is no way we can avoid complicity, and we can all think of specific times when we revealed our capacity to become barbarians ourselves.

Perhaps we were merely thoughtless or hurried. Once, pruning a hemlock hedge at the border of our property, I came across something I thought was an insect case affixed to a branch and with my clippers cut it in two. Then the horrible insight came: I had probably cut short the life cycle of a butterfly. I was stricken by remorse, but the deed was done, from sheer mindlessness. Even if it *had* been an insect case, did that give me permission for what I did? What did my action reveal about my belief in the harmony of nature? I wasn't paying attention. Full of *hubris* rather than humility, I had attempted to prune out of my garden those things that did not suit me. It seemed an insignificant event, but I was surprised by the pangs of guilt it produced. I suppose that was a sign of how much my consciousness had already been raised.

How do we respond to our predicament? We can become prisoners of our guilt, like the struggling insect becoming ever more entangled in the spider's weavings. Or we can acknowledge that we all have contributed to the world's suffering, express our contrition for what we have done and for what we have left undone, and then move on, with hope, towards the future.

We need not rely only upon words of penitence; each *action* of ours can contribute either to the communal sin of humanity or to its redemption. Our prayer for forgiveness can become incarnate through what we do and the way we live. Simple things, like turning off unnecessary lights, turning down the heat, turning over paper to use the other side, will be the signs our hearts have turned toward God with repentance and with hope. I was amazed the other day while binding up newspapers for recycling to find the hymn "St. Patrick's Breastplate" starting to ring in my ears. When I thought about it, I realized the phenomenon was not at all surprising, because my action was like a liturgical action, expressing my prayer for the earth and my desire to contribute to her healing:

> ...I bind unto myself today
> the virtues of the starlit heaven,
> the glorious sun's life-giving ray,
> the whiteness of the moon at even,
> the flashing of the lightning free,
> the whirling wind's tempestuous shocks,
> the stable earth, the deep salt sea,
> around the old eternal rocks.

I bind unto myself the Name,
the strong Name of the Trinity,
by invocation of the same,
the Three in One, and One in Three.
Of whom all nature hath creation,
eternal Father, Spirit, Word:
praise to the Lord of my salvation,
salvation is of Christ the Lord.

Spadework

Who are the "barbarians" who come to your mind? Perhaps they are people in positions of power with whom you disagree, or ordinary people whom you think are ignorant or thoughtless. Are there any aspects of their behavior that you can observe in yourself? Do you think that any aspect of your life-style might be destructive to the well-being of the planet? Is God's forgiveness, with its assurance of new beginnings, a reality for you?

As an example, I find myself getting very angry when national leaders make decisions based on economic prosperity rather than environmental well-being. However, it was only in the last year that I found myself compelled by conscience to pay the extra cost of recycled computer paper on which to print out manuscripts like this one!

Prayer with words

Compose your own litany of penitence. For what do you need to be forgiven? For what does your nation need to be forgiven? For what does humanity need to be forgiven? Follow each petition with the response, "Creator, forgive us."

Prayer with actions

Using some of the many lists of "Ways to Save the Earth" as a resource, choose an action that will become your enacted prayer for forgiveness and also a sign of your hope in the future. Choose a simple thing—something you do regularly. Some suggestions: begin taking your own canvas bags to the grocery store to use in lieu of paper or plastic. If you do not yet have curbside recycling, make your regular trips to the local recycling center as a pilgrimage. Plant a vegetable garden. Choose bicycling or walking instead of the car whenever possible, and remember why you are doing it. Above all, be mindful that the action you have chosen is a way of prayer.

Once this association of prayer and action has become natural, add another action to which you will bring similar mindfulness. Gradually, build your own list, which will be like an enacted litany that will punctuate your daily life with prayer.

CHAPTER 17

Despair and Burnout

During the dramatic early days of the Persian Gulf crisis, I went to bed every night with mental pictures of warfare that I could not seem to exorcise no matter how I tried to drive them away. Violent images became interior monsters who cast a constant shadow. News of the destruction of human life and devastation of the natural environment gnawed at my joy, at my hope, and at my energy.

One evening during this period, I attended a ballet by a Japanese dance company. The performance was a dazzling blend of color, sound, and movement entitled, appropriately, *Mandala*. The story is set in the early Edo period in Japan, at the time when Christians were being persecuted. The principal characters are Moe, a young woman who was a secret Christian, and Hokuba, a young painter who is working on a great mandala, a circular religious painting representing the cosmic order. Hokuba's mandala is filled with many figures, and he wishes Moe to pose for the central figure. In a climatic scene, the figures in the mandala come to life, and dancers in brilliant costumes move against the golden backdrop of Hokuba's great project. It was a scene from another age, another place, another time, another world.

As I lay my head on the pillow that evening, I noticed a difference in myself. My head swam with images of golden kimonos, colorful sets, the exhilaration of sound and movement. Shining pictures of beauty had, for a time, banished the ugly vision of war. The artist Hokuba's mandala had fulfilled its destiny as symbol of universal harmony for this member of the audience, at least.

It is no mere chance that the word "imagination" is derived from *imago*, "picture," because our thoughts often appear in the form of mental pictures. When we imagine the future, we picture it. When we remember the past, we see mental home movies of past events.

My experience with *Mandala* showed me that images play an important role in dealing with present reality as well. They have tremendous power because they are the language of the unconscious mind; our dreams are more likely to resemble an evening at the cinema than an afternoon in the lecture room. Moreover, images often slip unbidden, and sometimes unwanted, into our unconscious mind, a fact much appreciated by the world of advertising.

If this is so, it is no more self-indulgent to provide our imaginations with a balanced diet of images than it is to feed our bodies with healthy food. The media show us the most dramatic events in the world and these are often fearful. But these images do not represent the real world in all its fullness, so if we receive these alone, we fill ourselves with a distorted reality. The counterbalance can be discovered in those less newsworthy situations around the world: the compassionate work of the nursing staff in a hospice; the millions of second-graders on swingsets and see-saws at recess time at any given moment; the acres of wilderness where the only sounds are those of birdsong, brook, and the wind in the birches; the beauty of a ballet; a mental picture of Jesus healing a blind man.

When we forget the need to balance negative images with positive ones, we are inviting spiritual indigestion. We are disregarding nutrition just as much as if we believed ourselves compelled to gobble down whatever food happened to catch our attention as we walked along a city sidewalk—candy bars, frozen yogurt, bagels, shishkebab, hot dogs, hot pretzels, roasted chestnuts—and never chose our own meals.

The pictures we carry in our imaginations have the power to form the future, for, in a mysterious way, collective thought is a channel of energy for good or for ill. That is why "faith" is not an abstract concept, but a practical reality. It is a matter of courage—keeping our *coeur*, our heart, beating despite the seductiveness of depression, burnout, and despair. It is a matter of guarding our joy.

It is common knowledge that a person who is ill can become better by picturing "wellness," whether it be through imagining the shrinking of a tumor or the lowering of blood pressure. Similarly, when we furnish our minds with images of beauty and of wholeness, of "God's kingdom come" in the world around us, we surely contribute to the health of the earth, as well as our own ability to work, with all our energy, all our intelligence, and all our imagination on its behalf.

Surely God means us to take delight in the dance of life—the sparrows chattering at the birdfeeder, the forsythia branches bursting into sunshine, the fugues of Bach, the cry of the loon, the warmth of human affection—even as we rage at injustice. God means us to use that rage to right wrongs rather than to become spiritually unglued. God means us to care for our physical and our spiritual vitality, and to keep things in perspective.

The negative images we see are all too real, but despair is not the only option. The monk and writer Thomas Merton reminds us of the other reality, which is the mandala, the vision of God:

The more we persist in misunderstanding the phenomena of life, the more we analyze them out into strange finalities and complex purposes of our own, the more we involve ourselves in sadness, absurdity and despair. But it does not matter much, because no despair of ours can alter the reality of things, or stain the joy of the cosmic dance which is always there.[26]

Spadework

What powerful positive images—from Scripture, nature, the arts, or your experience—might you draw upon when you are overwhelmed with depression or despair? For example:

—Picture yourself doing something you like to do, such as swimming, running, or dancing—or, better still, go out and do it.

—Use images from Scripture. Imagine yourself donning St. Paul's "whole armor of God"—the belt of truth, the breastplate of righteousness, the shoes of peace, the shield of faith, the helmet of salvation, and the sword of the Spirit—in order to guard your joy.

—Picture yourself being carried by the Good Shepherd, or as one of the multitude in the story of Jesus feeding the five thousand.

—Say the service of Compline, which concludes with the antiphon, "Guide us waking, O Lord, and guard us sleeping; that awake we may watch with Christ, and asleep we may rest in peace."

Use an imaging prayer for healing. First, choose an environmental situation that especially distresses you. Perhaps it is a polluted stream or garbage-strewn vacant lot near your home; perhaps it is something you have seen on television, such as a wetland being drained for condominiums or a forest threatened with destruction. However, when you first practice this exercise, it is best to begin with something local with which you are very familiar.

Spend some time relaxing and breathing slowly and deeply, and then picture the place in as much detail as you can, using all the senses. What aspects of the scene are unhealthy? Is there potential for health? Perhaps you are picturing an urban vacant lot that has become an eyesore, full of rubbish. But the lot has good soil, and it is near a local elementary school.

Can you envision the vacant lot restored to health? How would it look? Perhaps you will picture a garden planted with vegetables and flowers, or a small grassy park with paths and comfortable benches.

Ask God to help you envision ways in which the change can come to pass. Perhaps the vacant lot could be the special project of a school class. The lot would be cleared of debris and the soil tilled by some willing adults. The children would be guided by an experienced gardener, who would help them with planning and planting. They would then take responsibility for tending it. It would be transformed from an eyesore into a place of which the community could be justly proud.

VI.

Harvest

A ll winter long we pore over seed catalogs that beckon us toward a vision of the garden as we would like it to be. Seldom does the gardener see the perfect garden of the seed catalogs, but the vision remains. We work towards it, so that once in a while we can have the joy of glimpsing perfection—a particularly fine duet of color and texture in the campanula and sea-holly patch, a pink rose glimpsed through some lacey coral-bells, an enormous blue Hubbard squash beside ripening cherry tomatoes, a perfect row of lettuce, a shiny canopy of basil.

A prominent theme in the Christian scriptures is the vision of the kingdom of God. When I was a seminary student, I learned with delight the phrase "already but not yet." Jesus and his followers believed the kingdom to be already here, because of God's incarnate presence among humanity, but not yet complete, because all people did not yet walk the way of love. The kingdom was, and obviously continues to be, "already but not yet."

That is the perpetual state of our garden, and it is the perpetual state of our lives as well. There are moments when we are privileged to glimpse the kingdom of God, sweet and surprising as the first red raspberry at harvest time. Like the raspberry, these moments are a foretaste of what the harvest might be if, with our cooperation, God's kingdom did indeed come on earth as it is in heaven. They might be glimpses of goodness, of unity, of renewal, of holiness in ordinary things. These glimpses reassure us that the harvest is God's, and that, in the end, all will be well and all manner of things will be well.

CHAPTER 18

Heaven and Earth are Full of Your Glory

A few years ago, I added something to my celebration of the Resurrection. After the Easter services at church, I went to the zoo with a five-year-old friend named Davidas. I found that I needed to remind myself that the earth celebrates the Resurrection too, and I wanted to be connected with creatures other than clergy, choirs, and congregations.

Since his father is Indian, Davidas was given a Hindu name meaning "servant of the divine," which also reminded his parents of the Hebrew "David," meaning "beloved." Davidas lives up to his name. When he was three, his parents told me, he had looked up at them during a trip to the zoo and asked, "Daddy, who made all these animals?" "God," his father answered, at which Davidas responded, "I really love God!" It was natural I should ask him to come with me to the zoo on Easter day.

As we strolled down the path to the zoo under the filmy canopy of new green foliage, we spotted some narcissus beginning to poke up through the brown earth. We walked to the sea-lion pool and stood there for almost half an hour, watching the graceful creatures splash and play and a mother sea lion stretched out on a high rock, nursing her baby. We made our way to the monkey house and spent another half-hour delighting in the tiny capuchin monkey's graceful gymnastics. We looked wonderingly at an exquisite baby giraffe, the carbon copy of its elegant mother, petted the sheep at the children's zoo, and peeked at the little foxes curled up in their den.

On a wooded path between the giraffe house and the aquatic birds, Davidas suddenly invented an impromptu poem that I recorded on the spot in a notepad I had tucked in my purse: "I hear the hawks calling, the birds singing, the feet of the animals. Nature is eating." The afternoon itself felt extraordinary—not as if we were living in ordinary human time, but in God's time. For a while, I lost my belief that the human species and its concerns stood at the center of the universe. While we licked ice cream cones from the zoo refreshment stand before heading back home, I realized that we had been, for a period, in Eden: in community with the sea lions, the capuchin monkeys, the baby giraffe, the sheep, and the small foxes. We were one with all "nature, eating."

God calls us to work and to pray for a restoration of the harmony originally intended for this earth. It is quite clear that Davidas hears this call, for this same child was asked by his first-grade teacher to write a composition about his favorite daydream. While his friends happily leaned over their desks scribbling lines about the acquisition of backyard swimming pools or new bikes, Davidas wrote this: "Wons I had a daydream that I wontid to save the animals from ikstikhion. And gat rid of the polohon [pollution]. And make the world lok bydfol [beautiful]."

Now seven, he recently informed me that his favorite animal was one of which I had never heard: a Jackson's chameleon. "It is a very wonderful animal! It lives only one place in the world: in the forest in Madagascar. When it is happy, it is medium green. When it is sad, it becomes dark green. But when it gets very angry, it becomes *black*. It is one foot long! And now it has less and less place to live, because people are cutting down the rainforest."

The desire to restore and heal the earth can be the fruit of a trip to the zoo, the tending of a garden, or the enthusiastic study of a chameleon. They are all openings to the wonder of God's creation. Awe, joy, and love are the powerful natural ingredients that will make this harvest come, in the end, organically, like a celebration.

I will never forget participating, quite by chance, in an event that reassured me that such a restoration of the earth's wholeness might still be a possibility, if only human hearts could be changed. I was showing a German friend the sights of New York City, and we had decided to visit the Cathedral Church of St. John the Divine for its St. Francis Day service of worship. I had intended to sit with her in the congregation, but I was spotted by a fellow priest who lost no time in enlisting me as a participant in the service, since, by coincidence, several of his colleagues declared they had other engagements on St. Francis Sunday.

Thus it was that, when the organ began to play the processional, I was among the clerics who began walking down the aisle of that vast cathedral. I could not help noticing, as I glanced out of the corner of my eye, that the congregation was decidedly unusual—approximately a third of them were dogs. As dancers moved through the space of the transept

crossing, the choir, organ, and instrumental ensemble wel-
comed us all:

> All praise be yours through Brother Sun,
> All praise be yours through Sister Moon,
> By Mother Earth my Lord be praised,
> By Brother Mountain, Sister Sea,
> Through Brother Wind and Brother Air,
> Through Sister Water, Brother Fire
> The Stars above give thanks to Thee.
> All praise to those who live in peace.
>
> All praise be yours through Brother Wolf,
> All praise be yours through Sister Whale,
> By Nature's song my Lord be praised,
> By Brother Eagle, Sister Loon,
> Through Brother Tiger, Sister Seal,
> Through Sister Flower, Brother Tree
> Let Creatures all give thanks to Thee.
> All praise to those who live in peace.
>
> Ask of the Beasts and they shall teach
>   thee the beauty of the Earth.
> Ask of the Trees and they shall teach
>   thee the beauty of the Earth.
> Ask of the Flowers, they shall teach
>   thee the beauty of the Earth.
> Ask of the Winds and they shall teach
>   thee the beauty of the Earth.
>
> For the Beauty of the Earth, Sing, Oh Sing Today,
> Of the Sky and at our birth, Sing, Oh Sing Always,
> Nature, Human and Divine, all around us lies,
> Lord of All to Thee we raise grateful hymns of praise.[27]

We heard the paean to love from the Song of Solomon, a portion of Paul's letter to the Galatians, and Matthew's admonition to consider the lilies of the fields. The bishop preached; I do not remember what he said, but I remembered his down-to-earth style and inspired common sense. We joined in the Nicene Creed: "We believe in one God...maker of heaven and earth, of all that is, seen and unseen...." We prayed for "the good earth which God has given us, and for the wisdom and will to conserve it." The bishop moved into the Great Thanksgiving: "God of all power, Ruler of the Universe, you are worthy of glory and praise....At your command all things came to be: the vast expanse of interstellar space, galaxies, suns, the planets in their courses, and this fragile earth, our island home." In response to this mystery, the music of the Sanctus rose toward the vaulting: "Holy, Holy, Holy Lord, God of power and might, Heaven and earth are full of your glory...." We prayed to be delivered from the presumption of "coming to this Table for solace only, and not for strength; for pardon only, and not for renewal," so that we could, by the grace of the Holy Communion be made "one body, one spirit in Christ, that we may worthily serve the world in his name."

Clergy received the bread and the wine and then distributed it to communicants with the accompaniment of an "Agnus Dei" of harp seal sounds, piano, cello, saxophone, and human voices, and a communion anthem that featured the haunting call of the spotted owl. Small children wandered in and out of chapels holding pet guinea pigs, and the dogs and cats in the congregation, sensing the tranquility, were peaceable.

Finally, the bishop, standing tall, made an announcement: "Now be very silent, and please do not take flash pictures." A deep hush fell upon the cathedral, and the great bronze doors at the west end swung open to another procession, more elegant by far than ours had been. Led by bright banners representing the four elements of creation—air, water, earth, and fire—the creatures came, both great and small. A llama. A bald eagle. A New York city rat, safe in its cage. A hedgehog. A jar of microbes. A camel. A sheep. Snakes curled in a box. And finally, in great and solemn dignity, an elephant. They formed a living circle around the bishop, who blessed them, one by one.

Afterwards, I made my way to the spot on the cathedral green where I had been instructed to stand near some tables covered with information about various environmental organizations. People were getting together around those tables, looking at the pamphlets, signing petitions, and exchanging information. Others had joined one of the several queues of pets and their owners, waiting for the second animal blessing to begin. I took my place. Dogs with limpid eyes looked up into my own and cats shyly peeked from under their owner's coats to receive their benediction. I placed my hand in blessing on two crabs, a rabbit, several guinea pigs, and two boa constrictors. But it was really I, myself, who was blessed.

I was blessed by hope. I had witnessed a great cathedral helping people to make the connection between the pets that they loved already and the broader sphere that they could be drawn to love: the entire creation. I saw a New York crowd remarkable for its peacefulness and happiness, an urban scene that was just as powerful as the violence that is more often in the limelight. I saw people's minds and imaginations engaged in discovering ways to make the world better. Most of all, I saw the whole enterprise flowing organically out of worship and prayer, calling upon not merely human power, but the power of God.

It felt like a bountiful harvest, a foretaste of God's kingdom, and I found myself remembering the prayer of thanksgiving that had brought our worship to a close in the great cathedral beside us. That prayer sent us forth from the sacred space designed by architect and artist to a greater sacred space—the earth—where our worship would continue, an outpouring of our wonder and our love.

We give you thanks most gracious God, for the beauty of earth and sky and sea; for the richness of mountains, plains, and rivers; for the songs of birds and the loveliness of flowers, and for the wonder of your animal kingdom. We praise you for these good gifts, and pray that we may safeguard them for our posterity. Grant that we may continue to grow in our grateful enjoyment of your abundant creation, to the honor and glory of your Name, now and for ever. Amen.

Spadework

Have you experienced moments of unity with other creatures? Did those moments feel like glimmers of the kingdom of God? Have you ever taken part in any worship similar to the St. Francis celebration at the cathedral? Can you think of some simple ways to include the rest of creation in worship, perhaps through prayers or music?

Making special journeys or pilgrimages of prayer to holy places is something people have done for centuries. Often they erect "stations" to mark their journey. They might commemorate particular events, such as the Stations of the Cross, helping the worshiper to reflect on the events of Good Friday. One sometimes sees these stations as bas-reliefs on the walls of a church.

You can also devise your own stations that help you to reflect upon something in nature. I did this once on a hike in the mountains, pausing to meditate at the side of a brook, on a high rock in the warm sun, and at the edge of a flower-covered meadow.

Create your own stations based upon nature.

Perhaps you have a back yard. Your first station could be the step outside the back door, where you thank God for the beauty of the outdoors. Then you might move to a spot underneath a tall tree, in which you recognize the spirit of *viriditas*, God's power for green growth. Looking into a flower bed, you can stand in awe of the infinite variety of color and species in nature. By the compost heap, you can place your sorrows and grievances in God's hands. Beside a newly sprouted plant, thank God for the reality of the resurrection life. If there is a birdbath, reflect upon the renewing and cleansing power of water. By the fence, you can pray for God's protection. Seated in a lawn chair, let yourself rest in God's presence. Use your imagination. The possibilities are endless.

If you do not have a back yard, you can create similar stations in a park, or even on the sidewalk. There is always the sky above—it can be the station of God's overarching love—and the fire hydrant would make an excellent substitute for the birdbath. There are pigeons, and often shrubs or trees. And there are the many wonderful human touches one can find in a city—the pot of flowers glimpsed on a windowsill, the birdfeeder outside the fire escape, and the playground filled with children.

You can pray your stations beside animals in a zoo, plants in a botanical garden, or displays in a natural history museum. You can even pray your stations in your imagination, *picturing* the places you might visit.

Since all heaven and earth are full of God's glory, your life could well be seen as an unending series of stations where you celebrate the holiness and beauty of creation.

CHAPTER 19

Easter

When I was five, the high point of Easter for me was the privilege of standing on the chancel steps in the big church with the other members of the children's choir and belting out "The Little Flowers Came Through the Ground." Our director, who always wore a red hat on Sundays, had rehearsed us all during Lent, and by now we had no doubts about the text. Dressed in red choir vestments, freshly laundered and ironed by our dutiful mothers, we presented the congregation with our Easter message: "The little flowers came through the ground, at Easter time, at Easter time; they raised their heads and looked around, at happy Easter time."

For years afterward I thought the song was silly. How could little flowers, lovely as they might be, possibly serve as a metaphor for the wondrous resurrection of Christ? Wasn't the first Easter a unique event, with no parallels either in nature or human history?

Recently, I have begun to soften. Perhaps behind the childish words lay a deeper truth. Perhaps Easter draws our attention to the fact that we also are meant to be part of the earth's cycle of endless renewal. What if these flowers have been part of God's message to us all along? What if humanity is the only part of creation to resist the rhythms of the seasons of life, despite God's promise of renewal?

The frog does not complain, "I wish winter were over," but waits for the warm breath of spring to release him from the mud at the bottom of the pond. The grizzly bear does not growl, "I wish I were younger," but lumbers about her business of caring for progeny, seeking food, avoiding, if possible, her human predators. The little flowers of the children's song seem content to carry on their existence as quite ordinary brown bulbs for a good half of the year. These creatures are at peace with time and with seasons; they "know" Easter, in the way only reptiles, mammals, and the blossoming bulbs of spring can know it.

Harvest time in the garden helps me understand the relationship between Easter and another great festival of the Christian community, which comes in the dead of winter, near the very shortest day of the year. When the harvest is over and Advent snow is upon the garden, it seems as if nothing is happening. Instead, in the dark earth, seeds gestate and receive energy for new life, just as the world above is preparing for Jesus' birth. Later, in the liturgies of spring time, we will remember that, in his dying and rising, he overcame death. But already, in December, we are introduced to that mystery.

It is illuminating that we celebrate his birth at this season of apparent lifelessness. It is the time of the solstice, the threshold of the year. It is in the bleak midwinter that the child is born who will embody the promise of new beginnings in the midst of apparent death.

This same season marks the birthday of a departed friend, so the mystery of death is much on my mind. My eighty-nine-year-old mother tells me that this loss of mine is only the beginning: few of her old friends are still alive. We both can understand the words of Wendell Berry, poet and essayist of the natural world:

> The longer we are together
> the larger death grows around us.

How many we know by now
who are dead!

...But that is bitter
only to the ignorant, who pray
it will not happen. Having come
the bitter way to better prayer, we have
the sweetness of ripening. How sweet
to know you by the signs of the world!²⁸

What signs of the world? I look at our garden. There, change is a metamorphosis, not a leavetaking. No molecule ceases to exist; it is reprocessed, becoming new energy.

The tulip bulb has hungrily gathered into itself every bit of summer sunlight. When the tulip's long leaves seem to sicken and die, it is really just turning in upon itself and becoming a hermit, following the example of the caterpillar who spins a cocoon in a branch overhead. Both wait during the silence of winter for the call to new life in the balmy air of spring.

A perennial flower like the old-fashioned bleeding heart seems to disappear towards the end of summer, but during the winter its roots are keeping silence underground. When the warm sunlight beckons, the bleeding heart comes out of hiding, pushing up green shoots that will support festoons of pink blossoms.

Even the annuals do not really disappear. If I do not pull them out for the compost heap, they make their own compost *in situ*, graciously providing fertilizer for next year's petunias and nicotiana. And it is quite probable that they have managed to sow some offspring who will surprise us, come spring, by shooting up between the flagstones of the patio.

In the vegetable garden, the squash vines begin to yellow as the days shorten, and the tomato plants hang heavy with fruit. The air is thick with the fragrance of ripeness; we cannot keep up with the harvest, and we threaten to leave baskets of zucchini on our neighbors' doorsteps, ring their doorbells, and run. The garden is a vision of lush decadence, like a civilization's last profligate fling before the fall of an empire.

I wonder if our physical bodies, formed from *adamah*, are annuals. In the natural scheme of things, after all, they are meant to become good fertilizer, to return to our "old brown earth," like the marigolds.

Because waste is not the way of nature, it is impossible for me to accept that the other, unseen part of ourselves, God's *ruach*, disappears. I suppose that, in that respect, we are perennials—with a difference. Imagine that there was only one cycle of seasons for the tulip: a year of growth and then decay that culminated with an eternity of springtime. Suppose that the tulip blossom, instead of decreasing in size and vigor, took splendid new shape in an everlasting spring.

If the little flowers of the children's Easter song had been asked to elaborate on their concept of the Resurrection, they might have explained it that way. If we observe them and the other denizens of the garden closely, we will find ourselves reading one of the books of God, a kind of natural scripture. "Every creature is a word of God and is a book about God," said the German mystic Meister Eckhardt. This is an insight shared by other great world religions:

> The other day I was walking along the river....I was suddenly aware of the sun, shining through the bare trees. Its warmth, its brightness, and all this completely free, completely gratuitous. Simply there for us to enjoy. And without my knowing it, completely spontaneously, my two hands came together, and I realized that I was making *Gassho* [reverently bowing in prayer]. And it occurred to me that this is all that matters: that we can bow, take a deep bow. Just that. Just that.[29]

Nature can teach us about sharing, about beauty, about diversity, about dying, about living, and about goodness, if we

but read her book. She invites us to the joy of the harvest, for
her pattern is the pattern of Easter:

> Now the green blade riseth from the buried grain,
> Wheat that in dark earth many days has lain;
> Love lives again, that with the dead has been;
> Love is come again, like wheat that springeth green.
>
> In the grave they laid him, Love whom men had slain,
> Thinking that never he would wake again,
> Laid in the earth like grain that sleeps unseen;
> Love is come again, like wheat that springeth green.
>
> Forth he came at Easter, like the risen grain,
> He that for three days in the grave had lain,
> Quick from the dead my risen Lord is seen;
> Love is come again, like wheat that springeth green.
>
> When our hearts are wintry, grieving, or in pain,
> Thy touch can call us back to life again,
> Fields of our hearts that dead and bare have been:
> Love is come again, like wheat that springeth green.[30]

Endnotes

1. George Maloney, *The Breath of the Mystic* (Denville, N.J.: Dimension Books, 1974), p. 5.

2. John Jeavons, "Sustainable Microfarming," an address at the "Earth and Spirit Conference: Honoring the Connections" in Portland Oregon, Nov. 15-17, 1991, on Audiotape XT-9 (Boulder, CO: Sounds True Conference Recording).

3. Hildegard of Bingen, *Book of Divine Works, with Letters and Songs*, ed. Matthew Fox (Santa Fe, NM: Bear & Company, 1987), p. 379.

4. Hildegard of Bingen, *Illuminations* (Santa Fe, NM: Bear & Company, 1985), p. 33.

5. Evelyn Underhill, *Practical Mysticism* (New York: E. P.Dutton & Co., 1960), pp. 90-91.

6. Hildegard of Bingen, *Scivias* (Santa Fe, NM: Bear & Company, 1986), p. 375.

7. Judith and Herbert Kohl, *The View from the Oak* (San Francisco/New York: Sierra Club Books, 1977), p. 14.

8. Diane Ackerman, *A Natural History of the Senses* (New York: Vintage Books, 1991), p. 27. I recommend this book as a valuable resource for prayer and reflection based on the natural world.

9. Kohl, pp. 73-74.

10. Vincent Rossi, "The Eleventh Commandment," *Sonflowers Discipleship Journal*, March 1979.

11. Jeanne McDermott, "Biologists Begin Eavesdropping on 'Talking' Trees," *The Smithsonian* (December 1984), pp. 84-92.

12. Teresa of Avila, *The Life of Teresa of Jesus* (Garden City, NY: Image Books, 1960), p. 127.

13. Frederick Franck, *The Awakened Eye* (New York: Vintage Books, 1979), pp. 5-7.

14. Frederick Franck, *The Zen of Seeing* (New York: Random House, 1973), pp. 7-8.

15. Ackerman, *Natural History*, p. 5.

16. Ackerman, *Natural History*, p. 191.

17. Inuit song from Elizabeth Roberts and Elias Amidon, eds., *Earth Prayers from Around the World* (San Francisco: Harper & Row, 1991), p. 21.

18. Frederic Burnham, "Telling a New Story" in *Trinity News* 38:2 (1991), p. 9.

19. Reinhold Niebuhr, *The Oxford Book of Prayer*, ed. George Appleton (Oxford: Oxford University Press, 1985), p. 96.

20. Phyllis McGinley, *Saint-Watching* (New York: Crossroad, 1982), p. 95.

21. Teresa of Avila, *A Life of Prayer*, ed. James M. Houston (Bodmin, Cornwall: Multnomah Press, 1983), p. xxv.

NANCY ROTH

22. Doris Janzen Longacre, *Living More With Less* (Scottdale, Pa.: Herald Press, 1980), p. 53.
23. Dorothee Soelle, quoted in Tilden Edwards, *Living Simply Through the Day* (New York: Paulist Press, 1977), p. 137.
24. C. P. Cavafy, "Waiting for the Barbarians" in *Perfected Steel, Terrible Crystal: an Unconventional Source Book of Spiritual Readings in Poetry and Prose* (New York: Seabury Press, 1981), pp. 190-91.
25. Roberts and Amidon, *Earth Prayers*, p. 66.
26. Thomas Merton, *The Monastic Journey* (Kansas City: Sheed Andrews & McMeel, 1977), p. 17.
27. Jim Scott and Paul Winter, "Canticle of Brother Sun" (Litchfield, CT: Living Music Records, 1982).
28. Quoted in Roberts and Amidon, *Earth Prayers*, p. 321.
29. Quoted in Matthew Fox, *Original Blessing* (Santa Fe, NM: Bear & Co., 1983), p. 109.
30. J. M. C. Crum, *The Hymnal 1982*, no. 204.